♦

NAMES
GAMES

♦

◆

NAMES
GAMES

◆

ANAGRAMS,
ACROSTICS, AND
PALINDROMES ON
FAMOUS PROPER NAMES

◆

Nicholas Morris

A DELL TRADE PAPERBACK

A Dell Trade Paperback

Published by
Dell Publishing
a division of
Bantam Doubleday Dell Publishing Group, Inc.
666 Fifth Avenue
New York, New York 10103

ISBN: 0-440-50360-4

Printed in the United States of America

Published simultaneously in Canada

May 1991

10 9 8 7 6 5 4 3 2 1

BVG

CONTENTS

v

INTRODUCTION

This may get me in trouble with the authorities, but I'd like to put in a word for daydreaming at the office. You see, one day about ten years ago I was doodling at my desk when I should have been writing press releases. For some reason, I scribbled down the name "Scarlett O'Hara" and began to shuffle around the letters to see if I could form any words. Imagine my delight when the letters rearranged themselves into the phrase "O Rhett, a Rascal." Since that day I have been an avid word-game fan and constructor. From anagrams I went on to palindromes and acrostics, and the result is the book you now hold, one that I hope will bring you many happy hours of linguistic merrymaking.

Names Games is an attempt to revive some neglected forms of wordplay, particularly the anagram, acrostic, and palindrome. These forms go back to the ancient Greeks, but apart from my palindrome on the battle of Salamis and my anagram of Oedipus Rex, the samples to follow have a decidedly contemporary spin. I have invented some new light-verse forms and created some brainteasing anagram and acrostic puzzles to challenge you. As the final touch I present a series of pangrams, or 26-letter sentences that use all the letters of the alphabet only once.

I thought you would want to know the historical background to these frivolities. Following is a brief summary of the wordplay used in *Names Games*.

ANAGRAMS

"Anagram" comes from the ancient Greek word "anagrammatizein," meaning "to transpose letters." As a simple illustration, "pots" is an anagram of "tops" (or how about my personal favorite: "slut/lust"). An anagrammatist rearranges the letters of the subject into a new phrase without deleting or substituting any letters. Ideally, the new phrase should reveal an appropriate message concerning the original subject.

Tradition honors a certain Lycophron, a Greek poet and dramatist of the third century B.C., as the first genuine anagrammatist. He lived in Alexandria during the reign of Ptolemy Philadelphus and was assigned the task of sorting the comedies in the great library at Alexandria, which his patron Ptolemy made famous. Lycophron's major surviving work is an iambic poem called *Alexandra,* which recounts the fall of Troy. Scholars have found two anagrams in the work, one on Ptolemy (translated as "made of honey") and the other on Ptolemy's wife, Arsinoe (translated as "Juno's violet").

The rest of the *Alexandra* reads like a surrealist poem, full of invented words, private jokes, and unexplained allusions. But with his anagrams Lycophron set the standards for all future wordsmiths. His two samples (in particular, "Juno's violet") fulfill all the requirements: The anagrams contain all the letters of the original name and make a just comment on the subject.

The medieval anagrammatists kept the flavor of Lycophron in their quest for the meaningful anagram. The best sample from this time is an anagram on the Latin version of Pilate's question to Jesus (John 18:38). *"Quid est veritas?"* (What is truth?) Pilate asks. The remarkable response: *"Est vir qui adest"* (It is the man before you).

Anagrams became something greater than mere alphabetical reassembly among the Jewish cabalists during the twelfth and thirteenth centuries. These scholars of mysticism believed anagrams revealed truth and worked miracles. The third book of their tradition, called *themuru*, describes their search for truth through the transposition of letters. For Noah's name in Hebrew they formed "grace," and from the name "Messiah" they made "he shall rejoice." The cabalists even believed that the ancient prophets created human beings out of dust by reciting letters in a particular order.

Perhaps the last word to be said about the religious nature of anagrams is the couplet penned by the Puritan divine Cotton Mather. It is a remembrance of his friend John Nelson, an early pastor in Boston:

> *His care to guide his flock and feed his lambs*
> *By words, works, prayers, psalms, alms, and anagrams.*

The Golden Age of anagrams arrived in the seventeenth century, when monarchs and court poets in France and England excitedly adopted the pastime. Louis XIII of France went so far as to appoint Thomas Billon his "royal anagrammatist," at a salary of 1,200 francs, which was bestowed on his wife and children following his death. In England, flatterers of James I turned his name, "Charles James Stuart," into "claims Arthur's seat." Even gifted poets such as George Herbert and William Camden were known to have succumbed to the anagram diversion.

These seventeenth century anagrammatists did not bother themselves that much about alphabetical constraints. They would happily drop an inconvenient letter, combine two *U*'s into a *W,* or add an extra letter or two to arrive at the anagram. In Mary Fage's *Fame's Roll* (1637), one finds more than four hundred biographical poems, each prefaced by an anagram. To silence critics, Mistress Fage prefaced the work with a poem defending her right to drop and add letters at will, concluding, "Try th'anagrams hereby, and then you'll say/Whether I've used all the helps I may."

William Drummond, in his "Character of a Perfect Anagram" (1711), declared that "In an anagram, there must not be fewer nor more nor other letters, but the same, and as many as in the name. Yet when the same letters occur many times in the name, then the omission of one or more is pardonable."

How far we are from the spirit of Lycophron and the marvelous "Juno's violet." If anagrams are to work at all, surely they must contain all the letters and only the letters of the original name. Obviously one should be allowed to add punctuation in the anagram message, but adding or deleting letters becomes the equivalent of allowing proper names into a round of Scrabble.

During the nineteenth century anagrams became enormously popular. Lewis Carroll found inspiration in verbal fancies of all sorts. He invented countless mathematical games and word puzzles; his version of "Florence Nightingale," with its grace and sonority, is a paradigm of the "elegant anagram":

FLORENCE NIGHTINGALE
FLIT ON, CHEERING ANGEL

It's safe to say that the modern English anagram was born with "Florence Nightingale." Writers after Carroll devised many entertaining samples:

THE TAMING OF THE SHREW
HER MATE WON THE FIGHTS
(Attributed to "The Evening Star")

THE ARISTOCRACY
A RICH TORY CASTE
(Attributed to Ess Ell, 1906)

WASHINGTON CROSSING THE DELAWARE
HE SAW HIS RAGGED CONTINENTALS ROW
(Attributed to "'Skeeziks," 1890)

Howard Bergeson's delightful book *Anagrams and Palindromes* contains scores of similar jewels from this time.

Names Games examines the biographical aspect of the anagrammatical art. I've assembled quite a cast of characters from history, fiction, and our own time, figures from culture high and low, Broadway and Hollywood, sports and literature, politics and science. You'll find them all twisted, scrambled, and reassembled. In the first section of the book, "Riddlegrams," you are given the anagram in a rhyming couplet, and you must come up with the name of the subject. I throw in a few freebies to help you catch on to my style of anagramming. The second section, "Magical Clerigrams," contains verse puzzles that I have specially created to test your verbal ingenuity. Based on the clerihew verses of E. C. Bentley, these trifles contain an anagram embedded in a short four-line rhyme. You are asked to come up with the anagram that completes the verse.

ACROSTICS

The traditional acrostic is a verse in which the first letters of each line spell the name of the subject of the poem. Occasionally acrosticians choose to hide the secret name in the final letters of each line or in a series of letters in the middle of each line.

Perhaps the most famous acrostic of all time is the so-called "emblematic acrostic" found in the catacombs of Rome. It is the symbol of a fish, marking the secret burial place of early Christians. The letters of the Greek word for "fish," I-K-TH-O-S, are an acrostic code for "Jesus Christ, Son of God, Savior" *(Iesous Kristos THeon Owos Soter)*. The early Christians, in an effort to keep their identities secret from the Romans, used this fish symbol to acknowledge themselves.

In our day the acrostic lives on in the double acrostic invented by Elizabeth Kingsley. These marvelous puzzlements combine the traditional crossword with an acrostic arrangement. When you have finished, the puzzle grid reveals a quotation from a literary work. They are to my mind the most satisfying of word puzzles.

For the third section of this book, "Couplet-Crostics," I have invented a new form of acrostic wordplay, inspired by the double acrostic puzzle. You are invited to solve a simplified form of the double acrostic, with the solution not being a literary quotation but a rhyming couplet, the first letters of which spell the name of the couplet's subject. I hope you will enjoy this newest version of the acrostic.

PALINDROMES

Many wordsmiths claim palindromes to be the stateliest and most elegant of the ancient word games. Indeed, these noble phrases, reading the same backward and forward, reveal a true alphabetical symmetry. They are particularly delightful to construct because you never know where they will lead you. You begin in the middle and work your way outward in both directions. You never know the full meaning of the palindrome until the last letters are placed on both ends. This is quite the opposite of the anagram, in which you have alphabetical limits set before you even begin.

Palindromes, like anagrams, stretch back to the ancient Greeks. Oddly enough, the first recorded palindromist, Sotades, lived under the reign of Ptolemy Philadelphus, along with Lycophron, the first known anagrammatist. Occasionally palindromes are referred to as Sotadic verses, in honor of their supposed originator. Alas, Sotades didn't get on too well in life. Because of his scurrilous attacks on the king and state, Ptolemy had him sealed in a box of lead and tossed off a cliff. A sobering lesson for all modern day palindromists.

Palindromes appear in the book's fourth section. Since *Names Games* is supposed to have a biographical flavor, I have composed several palindromes that famous people might have said, including some by characters you will have met in preceding sections. And I believe you'll be seeing the first-ever palindromes-as-puzzles, in which you'll get a chance to recreate my palindromes. I also offer you a selection of longer palindromes, ranging from thirty-five to fifty letters.

The best palindromes have a certain clarity and proclaim themselves with authority: "Able Was I Ere I Saw Elba"; "A Man, A Plan, A Canal—Panama"; "Madam, I'm Adam." They not only flow smoothly in both directions, but their statements are blessedly lucid. Because of the severe alphabetical constraints placed on palindromists, many have resorted to pure nonsense or contorted phrases populated by such convenient folk as Anna and Otto, to say nothing of ever helpful "Hannah." In my palindromes I try to stay away from these contrived constructions.

PANGRAMS

A pangram is a sentence that uses all the letters of the alphabet, ideally only once. A well-known pangram attempt is the sentence "The quick brown fox jumps over a lazy dog," loved by typing instructors everywhere. It comes in at thirty-two letters. But a perfect twenty-six-letter pangram is such a rarity that the *Guinness Book of World Records* compiles them. As a conclusion to *Names Games,* I present my twenty-six letter PDQ pangrams. The Guinness people didn't go for my use of PDQ, so I hope the case I make for its validity is convincing.

Getting back to Scarlett O'Hara for a moment. As I mentioned, she was the first anagram I ever made, while I was working as a press aide for the French West Indies Tourist Board. She inspired me to perfect my technique and go after a whole gallery of names. During this time my greatest fear was that others anagrammatists might be working in a similar vein. It was conceivable, I thought, that others might uncover the same message in the same name I was working on. Sadly, this worry proved true when I came across a book of samples from *New York* magazine's competition. The competition in question was devoted to anagrams, and two entries were letter-for-letter matches for two of my creations. One was "Woodrow Wilson," and the other was my beloved "Scarlett O'Hara." *Spy* magazine had been running a "Monthly Anagram Analysis" column by Andy Aaron, and I knew it was only a matter of time before one of my people appeared there. Sure enough, the March 1990 issue contains the anagram message "Lied to Reagan" (the subject of this anagram is revealed in the Riddlegram section).

I had to accept that there was some sort of anagram ESP at work, and it is only fair to acknowledge the work of others working independently.

Luckily I've only run across these three instances of mutual anagramming; the rest of the book is entirely original material. But should you find an earlier printed version of any of these word frivolities, please send it to me. And here's another challenge for you: If you devise a better anagram or palindrome on a name in this book, please do not send it to me.

One last word: I've written *Names Games* so that it may be enjoyed as a puzzle book or simply a collection of wordplay to be perused at your leisure. Unlike crosswords, where the whole point of the exercise is to fill in the grid, my handiwork does not entirely depend on the puzzle element. But I think you might have fun grappling with the puzzles, and I sincerely hope some of them can be done on company time.

RIDDLEGRAMS

$\blacklozenge$

$\lozenge$

Before we get into the puzzles, a brief word on anagram style:

Anagrams should not be mere rearrangements of words into other words. For the exercise to be at all profitable (to the creator and to you, the reader), the words, or in this book the names, need to be rearranged into a meaningful phrase, a message that relates somehow to the original subject. In creating anagrams, you begin by hunting around for a key word. In Scarlett O'Hara, "Rhett" is an obvious key word. You then make the remaining letters fall in line around this key word.

As you can imagine, the anagram form is tight. There's not much room to maneuver. You must somehow force and squeeze a given set of letters into a cogent message, without adding or subtracting any letters. If you're one letter short, or if you have one letter left over that you can't fit in anywhere, that's just too bad. Believe me, the game can be frustrating. For example, I felt I was well on my way to success with the name of Bryant Gumbel, our well-known morning news announcer. I had found a good key word, "banter." That left me with "my" and "glub." Now if Bryant had only been named Gimbel instead of Gumbel, I would have had the anagram "my glib banter." Alas, I couldn't substitute the *U* for an *I* to make the word "glib," and how that hurt. Maybe there is an anagram in his name somewhere, but I was too frustrated to start over. A similar disaster struck with "Samuel Beckett." If fate had been kinder by just one letter, I would have had "bleak, mute cast." I must admit that working on these anagrams has made me more sympathetic to those poor souls who get five numbers out of a six-number lottery drawing. So close, but all you get is the booby prize.

Perhaps to compensate for the unforgiving rigidity of the form, anagrams tend to assume certain stylistic characteristics that I find appealing. It's as if the anagrams were insisting to emerge and be heard. For instance, an adjective may be pressed into duty as a noun, or punctuation may be freely adapted to suit one's purposes, or a close-enough word may be substituted for the exact word in question. As an example of the last, consider Lewis Carroll's memorable "flit on, cheering angel." Literally this would picture Florence Nightingale as an angel who is flitting about emitting cheers, but in the context of this anagram, cheering really means "cheerful" or "one who brings good cheer." With "Gustav Mahler," I was toying with the construction "hear vast glum," which to me evokes listening to his long, melancholy symphonies. For one of the poets you'll find later on, I came up with the anagram "hot lady's man." The correct spelling of this would have to be "hot ladies' man," but I believe I can claim anagram license for the alternate possessive. Of course, you need to guard against overindulging in these stylistic licenses. What I don't tolerate, however, is adding on words that only serve to give you extra convenient letters to make your anagram. I'd rather live with the heavy-sounding "hear vast glum" than have some elegant phrase made out of "Maestro Gustav Mahler." I do think it's all right to use middle names or the middle initial, as they constitute an integral part of the name. And I suppose you have to allow titles of rank or nobility.

With this wholly personal manual to anagramspeak in mind, let's proceed to the first part of *Names Games,* in which you are given the anagram and asked to reconstruct the name. I present you with some short rhyming couplets, and you will notice that the end of the first line, or more often the end of the second line, is in capital boldface letters. This is the anagram message. Your job is to spot the original name in this anagram. The overall category, such as "writer" or "Hollywood," should be of some assistance, and of course the couplet itself may offer some clues to the subject's identity. As a further help I have supplied a series of dashes that indicate the length of the first and last names. Also, one letter for each name has been placed in its proper position. These letters will serve only to confirm your guesses.

Interspersed among the riddlegrams are some freebies, which should give you a break from puzzle-solving. Later, in the clerigrams, we'll reverse the process. You'll be given the name and will have to come up with the anagram. So sharpen your pencils!

SCARLETT O'HARA
O RHETT, A RASCAL!

LITTLE RED RIDING HOOD
I'D HIDE, ROTTEN OLD GIRL

This beast of the forest, though stopped and hobbled,
Still made you ask, **WHAT IF GOBBLED?**

_ _H_ _   _ _ _ _   _B_ _ _   _ _ _ _ _

CINDERELLA
CLEAN, IDLER!

Eschewing the drab, our sneaky false friend
Appeared at encampments **IN REDCOAT BLEND.**

$$\underline{\ }\ \underline{\ }\ \underline{N}\ \underline{\ }\ \underline{\ }\ \underline{\ }\ \underline{\ }\ \underline{\ } \qquad \underline{\ }\ \underline{\ }\ \underline{\ }\ \underline{O}\ \underline{\ }\ \underline{\ }$$

GEORGE WASHINGTON
SO ENGAGING THE ROW

THE GREEN MOUNTAIN BOYS
ETHAN'S ENTIRE YOUNG MOB

'Twas the "Era of Good Feeling"
Our young nation, reconciled.
Her charm so appealing
ONE LADY SO MILD.

$$\underline{\ }\ \underline{O}\ \underline{\ }\ \underline{\ }\ \underline{\ }\ \underline{\ } \qquad \underline{\ }\ \underline{\ }\ \underline{\ }\ \underline{I}\ \underline{\ }\ \underline{\ }\ \underline{\ }$$

WOODROW WILSON
O LORD, SO NOW W.W.I.

CALVIN COOLIDGE
A CIVIL CLOD GONE

"They tell us we're **DARN NEAR GOAL,**"
Said his handlers, reading a poll.

_ _ _ A _ _ _ _ _ _ A _

In Moscow our spooks let out one loud cheer
When told by their Chief that those **BUGS GO HERE.**

_ E _ _ _ _ _ _ S _

◆ MAY DAY IN MANAGUA ◆

The Iran-Contra hearings shed ratings sub-zero
When a senator called forth: "**ROLL IN TV HERO!**"

$$\_\ \_\ \underline{I}\ \_\ \_\ \_\ \_\ \ \_\underline{\ }.\ \ \_\ \_\ \underline{R}\ \_\ \_$$

You may not care that he's a godless pagan
But you should be aware that he **LIED TO REAGAN.**

$$\_\ \_\ \_\ \underline{I}\ \_\ \_\ \ \_\ \_\ \_\ \underline{E}\ \_\ \_$$

Not the most tactful liaison,
But what a **GRAND TALE, DON.**

$$\_\ \_\ \_\ \underline{A}\ \_\ \_\ \ \_\underline{\ }.\ \ \_\ \_\ \_\ \underline{A}\ \_$$

GLASNOST ANAGRAMS

MIKHAIL GORBACHEV
   HAIL HIM! (A KGB COVER?)

RAISA GORBACHEV
   O, HE GRABS CAVIAR

KENSINGTON PALACE ANAGRAMS

PRINCESS DIANA
   AND SIRE PANICS!

PRINCE CHARLES
   RICH PEER'S CLAN

NICHOLAS AND ALEXANDRA

He: LENIN: RASH LAD.
She: AN OX, A CAD!

He creeps about her mauve boudoir.
This filthy, **PRYING ROGUE, TSAR!**

_ _ E _ _ _ _ _   _ _ _ _ U _ _ _

RULE BRITANNIA

"You can never be too rich or too thin."
     —The Duchess of Windsor

WALLIS WARFIELD SIMPSON
SMALL WINDSOR WIFE—A SLIP

MARGARET THATCHER
MARCH AT HER TARGET

NEIL KINNOCK
KNOCK IN LINE!

LORDS NOW HAIL him—daft old birds!
Hold your tongue—**AH, NO ILL WORDS.**

_ _ _ _ L _ _ _ I _ _ _ _ _

FLORENCE NIGHTINGALE
(Homage to Lewis Carroll)
  FIT LEG, O LINEN CHANGER
  LINEN GANG FELT HEROIC
  FIE! NOT GANGRENE CHILL

What do we want with a double helix?
When we desperately **NEED AN ALL-GERM FIX.**

_ _ E _ _ _ _ _ _ _ L _ _ _ _ _

◆ SHAKESPEAREAN ANAGRAMS ◆

WILLIAM SHAKESPEARE
I SLASH PALE, WEAK RIME

ROMEO AND JULIET
"JOIN-ME-LATER" DUO

"Cassio, run!
DAME'S DONE."

_ _ _ _ _ _ _N _ _

T. S. ELIOT

"Immature poets imitate; mature poets steal."
      —T. S. Eliot

STOLE IT

Those smallish letters, can't you see,
Adorn the work of **SMUG, NICE ME.**

       __. __.   __ <u>U</u> __ __ __ __ __ __

In Wales they knew around he ran
And dubbed him so: **HOT LADY'S MAN.**

       __ __ <u>L</u> __ __   __ __ <u>O</u> __ __ __

◆ WILDEAN ANAGRAM ◆

THE PICTURE OF DORIAN GRAY
PRICE FOR TRADE: GAIN YOUTH

◆ TWENTIETH CENTURY BRITISH ◆
FICTION

Can you uncover the author's name in each of these three anagrams?

(Special Challenge)

AH-HA, MOST DRY!

TERSE FORM

WHO ME, A SMUG MASTER?

RENE DESCARTES
TENDRE CARESSE,
ACRE TENDRESSE

(Translation: "Tender Caress, Bitter Tenderness."
Nothing much to do with this famous French
philosopher, however.)

Properly engaged, he would not falter,
Sending **JEERS UP AN ALTAR.**

 _ E _ _ - _ _ _ _ _ A _ _ _ _

His memory was rather short,
This hypnotically **CALM, PURE SORT.**

 _ A _ _ _ _ _ _ O _ _ _

His savage music is to my liking.
I find it awfully **SAVORY, STRIKING.**

$$\underline{\ \ }\ \underline{\ \ }\ \underline{O}\ \underline{\ \ }\ \ \underline{\ \ }\ \underline{T}\ \underline{\ \ }\ \underline{\ \ }\ \underline{\ \ }\ \underline{\ \ }\ \underline{\ \ }\ \underline{\ \ }\ \underline{\ \ }\ \underline{\ \ }$$

Now that Agnes de Mille wasn't such a nice gal
When I heard her remark: **"CODA RAN ON, PAL."**

$$\underline{\ \ }\ \underline{\ \ }\ \underline{R}\ \underline{\ \ }\ \underline{\ \ }\ \ \underline{\ \ }\ \underline{\ \ }\ \underline{\ \ }\ \underline{L}\ \underline{\ \ }\ \underline{\ \ }\ \underline{\ \ }$$

Tomorrow midnight, we'll be through.
I agree it's been **A HARD "RING," CREW.**

____ _H_ ____ __ _A_ ____

ARTURO TOSCANINI
NO ART IN IT, CARUSO

OPERA ANAGRAMS II

LUCIANO PAVAROTTI
ON A RIP, I VAULT TO A "C"

To unseat this diva, who firmly holds sway,
Try if you will—**JUST LAND ON HER "A"**!

_ _ A _   _ _ _ H _ _ _ _ _ _

◆ OPERA ANAGRAMS III ◆

In Handel roles she's a lion
When she dons **HER MANLY IRON.**

__ __ R __ __ __ __ __   __ __ __ __ __ E

RENATA SCOTTO
A ROTTEN TOSCA

BROADWAY ANAGRAMS

Once he wrote some amateur skits
But now **HE PENS DEMON HITS.**

_ _ _ _ _ E _   _ _ _ _ _ _ _ I _

I decline to join the queue
To hear him **BLEND OLD, WEARY BREW.**

_ _ _ _ E _   _ _ O _ _ '   _ E _ _ _ _

A grand ovation you've just won
Aren't you proud, dear **SMILIN' ONE?**

_ _ I _ _   _ _ _ O _

◆ FASHION ANAGRAMS ◆

YVES SAINT LAURENT
A VENT RUINS A STYLE

For Vreeland's show (you may quote)
He **LENDS A RARE COAT.**

_ _ _ A _ _ _ _ _ _ _ _ _ T _

He found **ARDEN PRICIER**
But Revlon dicier.

_ _ E _ _ _ _ _ _ _ I _

ANDY WARHOL
ANDY HARLOW

(Note: Andy's first talky film shot at the Factory,
Harlot, was about Jean Harlow.)

This Manhattan Islander
Was known as **DIANA LAVENDER**

_ I _ _ _ _ 　　 _ _ _ _ _ L _ _ _

LEONA HELMSLEY
LONELY SHE-MALE

DOLT RAN DUMP—It's full of rot.
My advice to you is **DUMP DARN LOT.**

_ O _ _ _ _   _ R _ _ _

Maybe you don't always smell so sweet.
But life on the whole is one **SWELL TREAT.**

__ A __ __   __ __ __ E __ __

SMITH BARNEY, HARRIS UPHAM & CO.
RUMOR HIT MANY BEARISH CHAPS

ERNEST HEMINGWAY
HEY, TIGER NEWSMAN!

Of Truman no fan
This **MINOR REAL MAN.**

      __ __ R__ __ __ __   __ __ __ __ __ __ R

Nebraska plains, the wheat, and all,
The treasured past, **WHAT I RECALL.**

      __ I__ __ __   __ __ T__ __ __

This folksy title hit pure gold
And how! Oh, **BOY, A KEEN WAG SOLD.**

      __ __ __ E__   __ O__ __ __ __ __   __ A__ __

OPRAH WINFREY
O, WHEN I PRY FAR

Spokesmen quake, and rightly so,
When he **SLAMS AN ODD "NO."**

_ A _   _ _ _ A _ _ _ _ _

News 'round the clock, let's not pretend,
Will never fly, won't be a **TRUE TREND.**

_ E _   _ _ R _ _ _

◆ BRITISH ACTORS ANAGRAMS ◆

Some say this actress misbehaves
When she as **SAD AVENGER RAVES.**

__ __ <u>N</u> __ __ __ __   <u>R</u> __ __ __ __ __ __

Those Ealing films he undermines
(I've heard it said he **SANG CUE LINES).**

__ __ <u>E</u> __   __ __ __ __ <u>N</u> __ __ __

ROBERT DONAT
O ROTTEN BARD

LESLIE HOWARD
LEAD ROLE WISH

> *Corollary:*
> ASHLEY WILKES
>
> *WHY ASK LESLIE?*

LAURENCE OLIVIER
REAL LURE IN VOICE

◆ HOLLYWOOD ANAGRAMS I ◆

ORSON WELLES
   ROLE-LESS NOW

PEARL BAILEY
   ABLE PLAYER, I

Trapped in the ruins of Sodom and Gomorrah,
Where our daredevil hero **FINDS A HORROR.**

_ _ <u>R</u> _ _ _ _ _   _ <u>O</u> _ _

Honestly the critics couldn't be ruder.
How dare they call you an **INERT BROODER.**

_ _ _ _ <u>R</u> _   _ _   _ <u>I</u> _ _

OLIVER STONE
VET ROLE IS ON

Won the role of the young suitor
By asserting: **"SO I'M CUTER."**

_ <u>O</u> _   _ _ <u>U</u> _ _ _

My fans have endured, lo these years,
My charmless approach, **MY PERT LEERS.**

_ _ <u>R</u> _ _   _ _ _ _ <u>E</u> _ _

Although the critics slander few
Still their **REVIEWS ANGER YOU.**

_ <u>I</u> _ _ _ _ _ _ _   _ _ _ <u>V</u> _ _

33

◆ HOLLYWOOD ANAGRAMS III ◆

SYLVESTER STALLONE
ROVES TALENTLESSLY

◆

MAGICAL
CLERIGRAMS

◆

The reputation of E. Clerihew Bentley, British journalist and mystery writer, rests on one book—*Trent's Last Case,* which Agatha Christie herself called "one of the three best detective stories ever written." But comic-verse devotees remember Bentley for his "clerihews," the whimsical biographical verses he invented at the age of sixteen while studying at St. Paul's School in London. A clerihew is a four-line verse on a biographical theme, in which the first two and final two lines rhyme. Bentley's original clerihew:

Sir Humphrey Davy
Detested gravy.
He lived in the odium
Of having discovered sodium.

Here are further samples, two of my favorites:

George the Third
Ought never to have occurred.
One can only wonder
At so grotesque a blunder.

The digestion of Milton
Was unequal to Stilton.
He was only feeling so-so
When he wrote *Il Penseroso.*

The first line is usually the name of the subject, but sometimes Bentley added words, as in the Milton example above. The lines do not scan, as Bentley wanted to have a proselike quality to his verses. The non sequiturs and dottiness only contribute to the offbeat charm of these verses.

Bentley recruited like-minded compatriots at St. Paul's, including G. K. Chesterton, who contributed some inspired illustrations. Bentley's son Nicolas believed that his father's greatest joy was living to see the word "clerihew" included in the Oxford English Dictionary.

The clerihew in some ways is not as demanding as other verse forms. There are no complicated meters to remember, and with only four lines one could conceivably toss off a few before breakfast. But achieving that Bentley quirkiness is not easy. The master imposed few strictures, but he did feel that the clerihew should not be a strict, factual accounting of its subject. If a clerihew was too realistic, too true to life, Bentley would likely dismiss it. Here is one he wrote but later rejected on grounds of too much realism:

Louis Quatorze
Had a penchant for wars.
He sent Turenne to the Palatinate
With instructions to flatten it.

The clerihew format offered an attractive pedestal for my anagram capers. I have co-opted the basic clerihew structure, with its four-line, AABB rhyme scheme, but have added an anagram on the subject. The anagram appears at the end of the second or fourth line in the verse, which I've named "Magical Clerigram." I've designed the verse in such a way that the reader can create the anagram that completes the line.

I should say right from the start that I am not trying to duplicate Bentley's singular style. I am after something different with the anagram addition, although I have tried to keep a light, humorous approach.

Here are the directions for solving the anagram puzzles:

- In the samples to follow, you will see a famous name in capital letters (the subject), followed by a four-line verse containing several blank spaces. Each space corresponds to one *letter* of the anagram you are to make of the name. The blank spaces are so grouped to indicate the length of each anagram word, and appropriate punctuation has been inserted to help you.
- The name of the subject furnishes you with the letters to use in making the anagram. This subject generally forms the first line of the verse, but not always, as in the "Queen Victoria" example. But to steer you toward the letters of the name, I have arranged them in scrambled fashion underneath the verse, in two groupings. These are the letters to use in making the anagram, no others.
- The group of letters on the left is identified as the "Help Word." Rearrange these letters into a word and try to insert them into their proper place in the anagram line (use the dashes indicating word length to position the word properly). If you are acquainted with the popular syndicated word game Jumbles, this help-word step should feel familiar.
- The group of letters on the right, identified as "Remainder," obviously contains the remaining letters from the scrambled name. You must try to rearrange these letters into the remaining word or words of the anagram above. If the help word was not the rhyming word, try to locate the rhyming word first in the remainder. With the help word and rhyming word solved, you should be able to dispose of the few remaining letters easily. One last warning about the rhyming word: Remember that two words can make a rhyme for one, as seen in the Louis Quatorze clerihew quoted above ("Palatinate/flatten it").
- Pay close attention to the supplied clues on word length and punctuation. They will help you work out the anagram. Remember that one-letter dashes generally indicate the words A, I, or O. An apostrophe can mean a possessive *S* or it can indicate a contraction (I'm, she'd, don't, it's). Also look for common consonant and vowel combinations, such as ed, th, sh, ch, ly, ou, gh, ing, etc.

• Finally, try to get a reading of the anagram, what it might be trying to say. Does it look like it begins with a verb? Maybe then that verb ends in "ing" or "ed." As you do more and more of the clerigrams, you should develop an intuition about these finer points.

The anagram must of course contain all the letters of the subject. It must also fit in with the verse. There are probably an infinite number of combinations of the letter string, but you are looking for that one combination that rhymes and matches the length of the words indicated by the dashes. In other words, just any old anagram will not do. The anagram you are looking for has to make sense with the verse.

As I mentioned in the introduction, you are not required to grapple with the puzzles. You can skip to the answer section and enjoy the completed magical clerigrams as comic verse. I won't be offended.

CAST OF CHARACTERS

Degrees of difficulty

* = Easy
** = Medium
*** = Hard

- Laurence Olivier**
- Maggie Smith*
- Woody Allen*
- Ingmar Bergman**
- Oedipus Rex**
- Marquis de Sade**
- Isaac Newton***
- Albert Einstein**
- Louis Leakey***
- Queen Victoria***
- Horatio Nelson**
- Liddell Hart*
- Thomas Paine**
- Cornwallis*
- The Boston Brahmin***
- Maria Callas**
- Noël Coward**
- Agatha Christie**
- Anthony Trollope***
- Louella Parsons**
- Mies van der Rohe**
- Salvador Dali**
- Gertrude Stein***
- Alice B. Toklas*
- Marcel Proust**
- Madame Bovary*
- Marie Antoinette***
- The Mona Lisa*
- Howard Cosell**
- Joe Namath*

◆ FAMOUS ACTORS CLERIGRAMS ◆

LAURENCE OLIVIER

"Young Olivier's delivery
Will one day be silvery,"
Says my coach at drama school
Mouthing whom

— —————— —————— —————.

Help Word   Remainder
E V I C O   L U R L A N E E R I

MAGGIE SMITH

Maggie Smith
Uses elbows and hands to act with.
And her voice is a positive crime.
Won't someone please

——— ———— ————?

Help Word   Remainder
H I T S   M E G I M A G

DIRECTORS CLERIGRAMS ◆

WOODY ALLEN

Woody Allen
Drinks milk by the gallon.
In hope that soon he
Won't be thought __ __ __ __ __ __ __ __ __ __.

Help Word: Remainder
W E L D   O Y L A N O

INGMAR BERGMAN

Ingmar Bergman
Is a Strindberg fan.
Notwithstanding, the studio planner
Asked him to

__ __ __ __ __ __ __ __ __ __ __ __ __.

Help Word: Remainder
R I M G   R E B M A N A N G

◆ UNMENTIONABLE CLERIGRAMS ◆

OEDIPUS REX

Oedipus Rex
Denounced Mumsy, his ex.
"How low you made me stoop!
King was __, __ __ __ __ __ __ __ __ __?"

Help Word: Remainder
X S E   O P R U E I D

MARQUIS DE SADE

The Marquis de Sade
Applies too much pomade.
Just one reason, I claim,
He'd make a __ __ __ __ __ __ __ __ __ __, __ __ __ __.

Help Word: Remainder
E Q I R U S   S E A D M A D

ISAAC NEWTON

Isaac Newton
Left the part about the forbidden fruit in.
When told that that was no sign
Snapped, "I suppose you

__ __ __ __   __ __   __ __ __ __ __ __ __?"

Help Word: Remainder
S O N I C E   A W T N A

ALBERT EINSTEIN

Albert Einstein
Preferred,
"__ __ __ __ __   __ __ __ __ __ __ __,   __ __ __ __?"
He never really cared
For "$E = mc^2$."

Help Word: Remainder
L E E R A T   E S B N I N I T

LOUIS LEAKEY

Louis Leakey
Is quoted as having been cheeky:
"When I find a dig gets dull
Then __,   __   __ __ __   __   __ __ __ __ __."

Help Word:
K L U S L

Remainder
Y O I E A E

46

RULE BRITANNIA

QUEEN VICTORIA

When speaking on matters Victorian
The Queen became rather stentorian.
After throwing the occasional fit,
She'd ask,
"—, ——— — ———— ————?"

Help Word:
R E E V

Remainder
T O I N C U Q A I

HORATIO NELSON

Nelson found honor at the Nile
(Then he decamped for a while).
But when he reduced the French to zero,
They cheered:

— —, ———————'— ————!

Help Word:
T I S O N A N

Remainder
O H O L R E

LIDDELL HART

(Sir Basil Henry Liddell Hart [1895–1970] was a noted British military expert. He championed the belief in mechanized forces as a strategy of movement.)

Basil Henry Liddell Hart
Was sure he'd told his men to start.
Then why were they all standing still?
And who on earth had
— — — — — — — — — — —?

Help Word   **Remainder**
T H A D E L   R I L D L

THOMAS PAINE

Thomas Paine
Hates the reign.
Against the king's men
He __ __ __ __   __   __ __ __   __ __ __.

Help Word   Remainder
I S M A   O H P T A E N

CORNWALLIS

General Cornwallis
At Yorktown finds no solace.
With its back against the walls
The imperial __ __ __ __   __ __ __ __ __ __ __.

Help Word   Remainder
O N L I   W C S A L R

49

THE BOSTON BRAHMIN

The Boston Brahmin
Asked, "What's the hahm in
Being one, and not of the mob?
For
—'— ——, ———— ———— ————."

Help Word
R O B N

Remainder
H O S M A T H I T N E B

MUSICAL CLERIGRAMS

MARIA CALLAS

Maria Callas,
Vowing vengeance and malice,
Shrieked, "I cannot do the gala
For they say __ ____ ___ ___ _____!"

Help Word   Remainder
A R M   L I S A L A C A

NOËL COWARD

Noël Coward
In front of Porter cowered.
Although he never quite stole
He did in fact _____ ___ ____.

Help Word   Remainder
R A W D   N E C O L O

AGATHA CHRISTIE

Christie felt protective
Of her meddlesome detective
When she had to face

— —, — — — — — — — — — — — —!

Help Word
H I T R T A G I

Remainder
S A E A C H

ANTHONY TROLLOPE

Anthony Trollope
Gave himself a wallop.
"To finish the damned lot
I need

— — — — — — — — — — — — — — —."

Help Word
H E T R A N O

Remainder
L O N O P T Y L

GOSSIP CLERIGRAM

LOUELLA PARSONS

Louella Parsons
Reveals all star sins.
How cruel her scrawl!

— ————— ————— ———.

Help Word
S P O O N

Remainder
L E S A U L A R L

INTERNATIONAL STYLE CLERIGRAMS

MIES VAN DER ROHE

Ludwig Mies van der Rohe
Stood his buildings all in a row.
Office drones spend their lives
In these __ __ __ __ __ __ - __ __ __   __ __ __ __ __.

Help Word
R E D O M N

Remainder
S E H R A I E V

SALVADOR DALI

Salvador Dali
Knew a touch of melancholy
When a critic from Granada
Wrote: __ __,   __ __ __ __ __ __   __ __ __ __.

Help Word
A R V S L I

Remainder
A D O L A D

GERTRUDE STEIN

Gertrude Stein
Called her publisher a swine.
He admitted he'd only read bits,
And now he wants

__ __ __ __ __ __   __ __ - __ __ __ __ __.

Help Word   Remainder
T U G N E R   S I D T R E E

ALICE B. TOKLAS

("I was born in San Francisco, California."—the opening
sentence of *The Autobiography of Alice B. Toklas,* by
Gertrude Stein.)

Alice B. Toklas
Yearned to be yokeless.
She'd say she was born in Ohio
To show Stein's __ __ __ __   __ __ __ __ __   __ __ __.

Help Word   Remainder
K L A S C   E B A L O T I

FRENCH CLERIGRAMS

MARCEL PROUST

Marcel Proust
Needed a memory boost.
"*Allons*, let's pump it.

— — — — —, — — — — — — — —!"

Help Word
T E C M U R P

Remainder
L O A R S

MADAME BOVARY

Madame Bovary—
Her husband made the discovery.
"The cause of your dilemma
May be a — — — — — — — —, — — — —."

Help Word
R O Y A V

Remainder
D A M B E A M

◆ FAMOUS LADIES' CLERIGRAMS ◆

MARIE ANTOINETTE

Marie Antoinette
Offered them *gateau noisette*.
'Twas rich and thick and terribly sweet
And cheap—

__.__, __ __ __ __ __ __ __ __ __ __ __ __ __ __.

Help Word	Remainder
A T E M	N O T N A T E R E I I

THE MONA LISA

The Mona Lisa
Was put in the tower of Pisa.
During all this sad while
On her face __ __, __ __ __ __ __ __ __ __ __ __.

Help Word	Remainder
L I M E S	H A N O A T

57

HOWARD COSELL

Howard Cosell
Must be off his carousel.
Or maybe plumb out of his gourd
For he's asking,
"__ __ __ - __ __ __   __ __ __ __ __ __ __?"

Help Word	Remainder
C R O D E S	L A O H L W

JOE NAMATH

Joe Namath
For shameth.
In that stockinged gam
You're __ __   __ __ __ — __   __ __ __!

Help Word	Remainder
E J T	N M A O A H

COUPLET-
CROSTICS

O̲ne Friday in March 1934, Mrs. Elizabeth S. Kingsley (Wellesley, class of 1898) walked unannounced into the offices of the *Saturday Review* and submitted a new type of crossword puzzle that she had invented. The editor examined it over the weekend and quickly decided to introduce the puzzles to the magazine's readers. So was born the "double acrostic," and the new word game caught on quickly. For nearly twenty years Mrs. Kingsley never missed her weekly puzzle.

The double acrostic is similar to a crossword but is far more challenging and rewarding. The solver fills in clue answers, then transfers each letter of the answer to a numbered grid atop the clues. When all the clues are filled in and the letters transferred, the grid reveals a quotation from a literary work and the first letters of the clue answers spell the name of author and book. Solvers who were looking for more excitement than the traditional crossword puzzle could offer took immediately to the double acrostic. Mrs. Kingsley summed up the appeal to the editors of the *Saturday Review*: "There is a certain fun in the thrill of the puzzle, to be sure, but what is the goal? It dawned on me that a puzzle which stimulated the imagination and heightened an appreciation of fine literature by reviewing English and American poet and prose masters would be a puzzle with a goal." Today, Thomas H. Middleton continues the double acrostic tradition with his puzzles in *The New York Times*.

Mrs. Kingsley's invention was perhaps the most inspired of all acrostic puzzles. But her work is part of a long acrostic tradition. As I described in the introduction to this book, a classic acrostic is a poem in which the first letters of the lines spell out the subject of the poem. While most acrostic poems are tepid and dull, here is one classic poem by Lewis Carroll, which forms the ending of *Through the Looking Glass*. In the poem Carroll spells out the name of Alice Pleasance Liddell, who was the inspiration for Alice in Wonderland:

A boat, beneath a summer sky
Lingering onward dreamily
In an evening of July—

Children three that nestle near,
Eager eye and willing ear,
Pleased a simple tale to hear—

Long has paled that sunny sky;
Echoes fade and memories die;
Autumn frosts have slain July.

Still she haunts me, phantomwise,
Alice moving under skies
Never seen by waking eyes.

Children yet, the tale to hear,
Eager eye and willing ear,
Lovingly shall nestle near.

In a Wonderland they lie,
Dreaming as the days go by,
Dreaming as the summers die;

Ever drifting down the stream—
Lingering in the golden gleam—
Life, what is it but a dream?

Most Victorian acrostics didn't aspire to Carroll's aesthetic heights. They were essentially child's play. The Queen herself was said to be fond of them, and it is believed she even composed a few "for the royal children." Tony Augarde, in *The Oxford Guide to Word Games,* cites one example that has come down to us. The royal charges were asked to supply the answers to a series of clues. The first letters of the answers, read top to bottom, revealed a city in England, while the final letters, read bottom to top, told what that city was famous for:

A city in Italy	N A P L E S
A river in Germany	E L B E
A town in the United States	W A S H I N G T O N
A town in North America	C I N C I N N A T I
A town in Holland	A M S T E R D A M
The Turkish name of Constantinople	S T A M B O U L
A town in Bothnia	T O R N E A
A city in Greece	L E P A N T O
A circle on the globe	E C L I P T I C

Luckily, we have the Kingsley acrostics to keep us occupied and stimulated. Once you have become hooked on double acrostics, it's very difficult to get excited over regular crosswords. Nonetheless, many budding double acrostickers go through a period of rage and frustration when first grappling with double acrostics. Admittedly, they are tough to crack in the beginning. But after you have struggled through about a half dozen, you start to figure out the various stratagems. Suddenly, you can solve them.

The most astonishing thing about double acrostics is all the cross-referencing that takes place. You work back and forth between the clue answers and the grid. Say you know five or six answers out of a total of twenty. When you have transferred their individual letters to the grid, you will start to see words forming in the grid. You then start guessing at the half-formed words in the grid and continue working back and forth from the grid to the clues.

About midway through, you may get a glimmering of what the quotation is about, or you may be able to guess the author's name or title (which will supply you with valuable first letters to clue answers). As you hurry to follow up your hunches, you start to see which of your earlier guesses prove to be true. Finally there comes a moment when all is revealed, the solution pops up, and you just race through to the end, clearing up the odd bits.

For my money there is no more satisfying word puzzle around than the double acrostic. If you haven't discovered them yet, be sure to give Thomas Middleton a try. Persevere, and you'll be well rewarded.

With all this buildup, you may think I am about to spring some Kingsleyesque acrostics on you. Actually, I have something slightly different in mind, so I am going to leave you here for a while. But don't worry, we'll be using all the acrostic tricks I've just described.

Names Games started out with only anagrams and palindromes. After a while I began to wonder if there were any other ways to dispose of my famous names. I had just then stumbled across Middleton and found my inspiration. Would there be a way of modifying the acrostic concept to come up with something original?

Soon I discovered that the first and last name of a famous person could form the framework of a rhyming couplet. Here's how the theory worked out on paper:

If you took a famous name, you could compose a rhyming couplet on that subject, in which the first letters of each word in the couplet spell out the name of the subject. Furthermore, the first letters of the words in the first line would spell the subject's first name (with the second line spelling the subject's last name). Naturally, the completed couplet must make a suitable comment on the subject.

As a further refinement I decided to try to have at least one of the rhyme words be a word that had a particular association with the subject. To demonstrate what I mean, here's my couplet on "Martin Luther":

"More About Rome" Theses I've Nailed.
(Lord Understands This, He's Even Railed.)

The trick was to write a couplet that does its job apart from the acrostic wending its way through the two lines. But when you look closely you see the first letters of the first line spell "Martin," while the second line spells "Luther." Also, the rhyme word "nailed" fulfills the key association requirement.

I had collected about a dozen or so of these couplets when I realized they were missing an important ingredient— the puzzle.

Here is where we come back to Kingsley and Middleton. I decided to make the couplet the "quotation" of an acrostic puzzle. I would supply a series of clues, each letter of which was to be transferred to the quotation grid. Upon completion, the couplet would reveal itself. Then I remembered that in classic double acrostic puzzles the first letters of the clue words spell the author's name and title. Since my couplets were original (not literary quotations), I would need something else. The solution was to have the first letters of the clue words spell out an additional key association word on the subject.

So I have taken the most enjoyable elements of the classic double acrostic puzzle and modified them to accommodate my rhyming couplets. To help you get started, let me furnish step-by-step directions, as well as a few inside tips:

DIRECTIONS FOR SOLVING COUPLET-CROSTICS

Each puzzle contains a list of clues, identified by successive letters of the alphabet. You are to write the answers over the numbered dashes located next to each clue. Each dash represents one letter of the clue answer.

Below the clues is the quotation grid, consisting of dashes numbered consecutively. After you have completed a clue up top, transfer each letter of the answer to its correspondingly numbered dash in the quotation grid below. Remember that the dashes are numbered consecutively in the quotation so you can locate them easily. I should also point out that the quotation grid is set up in a stacking order. Each line of numbered dashes in the grid corresponds to one word of the rhyming couplet.

You probably won't know all the answers to the clues, but don't worry. The acrostic setup, as described earlier, allows you to work in two directions, back and forth from the clues to the quotation. To go from the quotation to the clue section, refer to the letter in lower case following the number of the quotation dash. This letter identifies the clue word. For example, a quotation dash marked "19d" means that dash #19 is found in the clue word labeled "D."

There are other acrostic tips to help you. Remember that the initial letters of the rhyming couplet spell the name of the subject. This is what you are working toward. With the quotation words stacked one on top of another, you should be able to see clearly the letters of the first and last names. For example, here's how Martin Luther would look if he were set up in the quotation:

MORE
ABOUT
ROME
THESES
I'VE
NAILED

LORD
UNDERSTANDS
THIS
HE'S
EVEN
RAILED

Also remember that the last words in each of the couplet lines rhyme. In the "Luther" sample, if you had completed

66

the "ailed" in "nailed" you might want to assume that the last word in the second line ends in "ailed" as well. Just remember that not all rhymes are as straightforward as nailed and railed (I've included a few tricky ones just to make you work a little harder).

The other acrostic hint to remember is the series of first letters of the clue answers. When read from top to bottom, these initial letters spell out a word or words having a particular association with the subject. If I had done up Martin Luther into a puzzle, I might have chosen the word "Devotional," for example. This would mean clue word A begins with a *D*, Clue word B begins with an *E*, clue word C begins with a *V*, etc. This key word can be of great assistance. It will indicate the general nature of the subject. It will also help you to double-check and confirm your guesses. The most important thing to remember is that the initial letters of the clues and the quotation words are not just random letters. They reveal the key word and subject's name. Try to work them out and you will save yourself lots of time.

The final thing you must do to have the couplet make sense is insert appropriate punctuation in the quotation grid. This means all punctuation, periods, commas, apostrophes, dashes, parentheses, etc. You're on your own here, so when you are finished you may want to compare your punctuation with mine in the "Solutions" section.

I encourage you to use all your reference works, including the thesaurus, almanacs, encyclopedias, etc. (And I assume if you picked up this book you probably have a well-stocked reference library at home.) I've tried to make the clues challenging enough without using obscure words or references. There is usually only one really obscure reference in each puzzle. For example, in one puzzle I ask you to name the architect of Trinity Church in New York City. Now, I don't expect many people to know that. I had to use it because it was the only way to finish up my letters. Still, you needn't write off an obscure clue. Should you transfer some of its letters back from the quotation grid, you may be able to work out the word just by using your sense of sound.

I must ask you to forgive one minor defect of my acrostics. Occasionally I am forced to use more than one letter from the same clue word in the same quotation word. For example, in a quotation word of seven letters, you may find that two of the dashes are to be found in clue word B. Ideally this should not happen, as it makes life easier for the solver. I have to do it, though, as my quotations average only around sixty letters. (By contrast, the classic double acrostic puzzle contains up to two hundred letters in the quotation.) I have tried to contain this to only one or two quotation words in each puzzle.

I hope I haven't utterly confused you with all my talk about numbered dashes and cross-referencing. Don't be too discouraged, as you should catch on quickly once you start doing the puzzles. I hope you enjoy this test of cultural knowledge and that you'll have a chuckle or two over the couplets.

CLUES:

A. 1966 play by Joe Orton

___ ___ ___ ___
40 60 1   48

B. Imaginary, deceptive

___ ___ ___ ___ ___ ___ ___ ___
49 10 19 31 7   58 24 38

C. Sport

___ ___ ___ ___
8   46 27 21

D. American poet (1899–1932), "The Bridge" (full name)

___ ___ ___ ___ ___ ___ ___ ___ ___
55 51 36 3   47 12 15 25 23

E. Absenteeism, hooky

___ ___ ___ ___ ___ ___ ___
45 29 61 9   33 2   18

F. Without content; unintelligent

___ ___ ___ ___ ___ ___ ___
5   39 50 26 11 56 20

G. Italian Renaissance princely family

___ ___ ___ ___
6   42 17 13

H. By chance, haphazardly

___ ___ ___ ___ ___ ___ ___ ___
59 35 44 14 30 57 41 54

I. Nymph who terrorized Odysseus, aided by the whirlpool Charybdis

___ ___ ___ ___ ___ ___
32 16 43 53 37 4

J. Santa's helpers

<u> </u> <u> </u> <u> </u> <u> </u> <u> </u>
28 52 22 34 62

QUOTATION:

1a	2e	3d	4i	5f	6g	7b

8c	9e	10b	11f	12d	13g

14h	15d	16i	17g	18e	19b	20f

21c	22j	23d	24b

25d	26f	27c	28j	29e	30h	31b	32i

33e	34j	35h	36d	37i	38b

39f	40a	41h

42g	43i	44h	45e	46c	47d	48a	49b	50f	51d	52j	53i	54h

55d	56f	57h	58b	59h	60a	61e	62j

COUPLET-CROSTIC #2

CLUES:

A. Lack, scarcity

__ __ __ __ __ __
11 17 52 24 23 6

B. Greek mathematician (305– 285 B.C.)

__ __ __ __ __ __
25 38 56 8 40 18

C. Authority to act for another

__ __ __ __ __
37 13 1 55 42

D. Conundrum, brainteaser

__ __ __ __ __ __
45 16 30 60 51 12

E. Circuit, range, sphere

__ __ __ __ __
44 15 20 35 58

F. "Fight the good ——" (Anglican hymn)

__ __ __ __ __
3 57 50 34 33

G. Diacritical mark

__ __ __ __ __ __
22 36 43 2 49 28

H. Sergeant (abbreviation)

__ __ __
10 26 21

71

I. "—— macabre"

$\overline{47}\ \overline{9}\ \overline{39}\ \overline{53}\ \overline{54}$

J. Feeble-minded, foolish

$\overline{32}\ \overline{46}\ \overline{4}\ \overline{48}\ \overline{41}\ \overline{27}\ \overline{14}$

K. Teeter

$\overline{5}\ \overline{29}\ \overline{59}\ \overline{7}\ \overline{19}\ \overline{31}$

QUOTATION:

1c	2g	3f	4j	5k	6a	

7k	8b	9i	10h	11a	12d	13c

14j	15e	16d	17a	18b

19k	20e	21h	22g	23a

24a	25b	26h	27j	28g	29k	30d

31k	32j	33f	34f

35e	36g	37c	38b	39i	40b	41j	42c

43g	44e	45d	46j

47i	48j	49g	50f	51d	52a	53i

54i	55c	56b	57f	58e	59k	60d

◆ COUPLET-CROSTIC #3 ◆

CLUES:

A. Antipathy, rancor

<u>68</u> <u>40</u> <u>7</u> <u>49</u> <u>31</u> <u>44</u>

B. Sacred Hindu
writing

<u>59</u> <u>22</u> <u>33</u> <u>13</u>

C. Military supplies

<u>16</u> <u>6</u> <u>69</u> <u>20</u> <u>42</u> <u>23</u> <u>37</u> <u>46</u>

D. Liege

<u>28</u> <u>38</u> <u>12</u> <u>24</u>

E. Relative of Yankee
Doodle Dandy (2
wds.)

<u>39</u> <u>61</u> <u>56</u> <u>18</u> <u>29</u> <u>52</u> <u>11</u> <u>17</u>

F. Van Gogh's brother

<u>41</u> <u>8</u> <u>21</u> <u>2</u>

G. French painter
(1780–1867), "Jupiter
and Thetis,"
"Apotheosis of
Homer"

<u>55</u> <u>3</u> <u>63</u> <u>45</u> <u>32</u> <u>25</u>

H. The West

<u>9</u> <u>1</u> <u>30</u> <u>58</u> <u>15</u> <u>62</u> <u>43</u> <u>48</u>

73

I. Requirement

$\overline{}$ $\overline{}$ $\overline{}$ $\overline{}$
14 65 27 34

J. Borough in southeastern England, capital of Suffolk

$\overline{}$ $\overline{}$ $\overline{}$ $\overline{}$ $\overline{}$ $\overline{}$ $\overline{}$
5 47 26 10 19 66 54

K. Stylish, nifty

$\overline{}$ $\overline{}$ $\overline{}$ $\overline{}$ $\overline{}$
36 53 60 64 50

L. Robber

$\overline{}$ $\overline{}$ $\overline{}$ $\overline{}$ $\overline{}$
67 57 35 51 4

QUOTATION:

1h	2f	3g	4l	5j	6c	7a

8f	9h	10j

11e

12d	13b	14i	15h	16c	17e

18e	19j	20c	21f

22b	23c	24d	25g

26j	27i	28d	29e	30h	31a	32g	33b

34i	35l	36k	37c	38d	39e	40a	41f

42c	43h	44a

45g	46c	47j	48h	49a	50k	51l	52e

53k	54j	55g	56e	57l

58h	59b	60k

61e	62h	63g	64k	65i	66j	67l	68a	69c

COUPLET-CROSTIC #4

CLUES:

A. Broadway composer, "Somewhere over the Rainbow," "Stormy Weather" (full name)

‾‾ ‾‾ ‾‾ ‾‾ ‾‾ ‾‾ ‾‾ ‾‾ ‾‾ ‾‾ ‾‾
46 25 69 40 6 22 76 9 56 62 55

B. Practice; operation; lawsuit

‾‾ ‾‾ ‾‾ ‾‾ ‾‾ ‾‾
29 50 73 57 14 44

C. U.S. architect (1802–1878), Trinity Church, N.Y.C. (last name)

‾‾ ‾‾ ‾‾ ‾‾ ‾‾ ‾‾
15 42 1 51 59 37

D. Small child

‾‾ ‾‾ ‾‾
30 10 77

E. French health resort on Lake Geneva

‾‾ ‾‾ ‾‾ ‾‾ ‾‾
18 3 43 33 80

F. Concerto conclusion

‾‾ ‾‾ ‾‾ ‾‾
38 27 68 5

G. Imagined place of
ideal perfection

$\overline{7}\ \overline{34}\ \overline{79}\ \overline{41}\ \overline{23}\ \overline{47}$

H. Supplying of land
with water by
artificial means

$\overline{13}\ \overline{26}\ \overline{64}\ \overline{31}\ \overline{58}\ \overline{70}\ \overline{52}\ \overline{74}\ \overline{2}\ \overline{21}$

I. Cooked (with a
hissing sound)

$\overline{16}\ \overline{49}\ \overline{32}\ \overline{75}\ \overline{17}\ \overline{66}\ \overline{67}$

J. Jot, infinitesimal
amount

$\overline{78}\ \overline{36}\ \overline{60}\ \overline{11}$

K. Terrifying, scary

$\overline{24}\ \overline{4}\ \overline{19}\ \overline{39}\ \overline{65}\ \overline{28}\ \overline{72}\ \overline{12}\ \overline{54}\ \overline{53}\ \overline{61}$

L. Terse, satiric
poetical statement

$\overline{20}\ \overline{8}\ \overline{35}\ \overline{45}\ \overline{48}\ \overline{63}\ \overline{71}$

QUOTATION:

1c	2h	3e	4k	5f	6a

7g	8l	9a	10d	11j	12k	13h	14b	15c	16i

17i	18e	19k	20l	21h	22a

23g	24k

25a	26h	27f	28k	29b	30d	31h	32i	33e	34g	35l	36j	37c

77

38f	39k	40a	41g	42c	43e	44b	45l					
46a	47g	48l	49i	50b	51c	52h	53k					
54k	55a											
56a	57b	58h	59c	60j	61k	62a	63l	64h	65k	66i	67i	
68f	69a	70h	71l	72k	73b	74h	75i	76a	77d	78j	79g	80e

CLUES:

A. Neither Dem. nor
Rep.

$\overline{}_{30}$ $\overline{}_{23}$ $\overline{}_{4}$

B. Initials of your
author (See
copyright page)

$\overline{}_{8}$ $\overline{}_{40}$ $\overline{}_{14}$

C. Author of *A Child's
Christmas in Wales*
(1954) (last name)

$\overline{}_{33}$ $\overline{}_{38}$ $\overline{}_{28}$ $\overline{}_{6}$ $\overline{}_{22}$ $\overline{}_{16}$

D. Albion

$\overline{}_{5}$ $\overline{}_{24}$ $\overline{}_{31}$ $\overline{}_{21}$ $\overline{}_{1}$ $\overline{}_{42}$ $\overline{}_{3}$

E. Muslim holy
month, marked by
solemn fasting

$\overline{}_{19}$ $\overline{}_{7}$ $\overline{}_{29}$ $\overline{}_{11}$ $\overline{}_{43}$ $\overline{}_{41}$ $\overline{}_{2}$

F. Catch sight of;
noted American
wordsmith

$\overline{}_{25}$ $\overline{}_{36}$ $\overline{}_{20}$ $\overline{}_{34}$

G. Equestrian's seat

$\overline{}_{27}$ $\overline{}_{15}$ $\overline{}_{26}$ $\overline{}_{9}$ $\overline{}_{13}$ $\overline{}_{39}$

H. "Order of the ——"

$\overline{}$ $\overline{}$ $\overline{}$ $\overline{}$ $\overline{}$ $\overline{}$ $\overline{}$
17 32 35 10 37 12 18

QUOTATION:

‾‾ ‾‾ ‾‾
1d 2e 3d

‾‾ ‾‾ ‾‾ ‾‾ ‾‾ ‾‾ ‾‾
4a 5d 6c 7e 8b 9g 10h

‾‾ ‾‾ ‾‾
11e 12h 13g

‾‾ ‾‾ ‾‾ ‾‾ ‾‾ ‾‾   ‾‾ ‾‾ ‾‾ ‾‾ ‾‾ ‾‾ ‾‾
14b 15g 16c 17h 18h 19e   20f 21d 22c 23a 24d 25f 26g

‾‾ ‾‾
27g 28c

‾‾ ‾‾ ‾‾ ‾‾ ‾‾ ‾‾
29e 30a 31d 32h 33c 34f

‾‾ ‾‾
35h 36f

‾‾ ‾‾ ‾‾
37h 38c 39g

‾‾ ‾‾ ‾‾ ‾‾
40b 41e 42d 43e

COUPLET-CROSTIC #6

CLUES:

A. Film preview

—— —— —— —— —— —— —— —— ——
30 44 59 55 10 23 16 50 41

B. Peace of ———,
concluding Thirty
Years' War

—— —— —— —— —— —— —— —— —— ——
11 48 21 25 51 45 2 7 36 58

C. Consequence

—— —— —— —— —— —— —— —— ——
43 54 27 29 9 1 60 46 12

D. An utterance that
"does not follow"

—— —— —— —— —— —— —— —— —— —— ——
19 47 40 5 52 31 28 13 38 65 53

E. Talkative

—— —— —— —— —— —— —— —— —— ——
15 35 64 32 6 56 39 22 18 63

F. More competent

—— —— —— —— ——
26 61 8 4 14

G. Living; sustenance;
stronghold

—— —— —— ——
3 62 33 34

H. He "never really
cared for E=mc²"

—— —— —— —— —— —— —— ——
42 20 17 24 57 66 49 37

QUOTATION:

| 1c | 2b | 3g | 4f | 5d | | | | | |

| 6e | 7b | 8f |

| 9c | 10a | 11b | 12c | 13d | 14f | 15e |

| 16a | 17h |

| 18e | 19d | 20h | 21b | 22e | 23a |

| 24h | 25b | 26f | 27c | 28d | 29c | 30a | 31d | 32e | 33g |

| 34g | 35e | 36b | 37h | 38d | 39e | 40d | 41a |

| 42h | 43c | 44a | 45b |

| 46c | 47d | 48b |

| 49h | 50a |

| 51b | 52d | 53d | 54c | 55a | 56e | 57h |

| 58b | 59a | 60c | 61f | 62g | 63e | 64e | 65d | 66h |

COUPLET-CROSTIC #7

CLUES:

A. Monastery; arcaded passageway

___ ___ ___ ___ ___ ___ ___ ___
15 34 12 27 41 30 61 57

B. An open declaration or acknowledgment

___ ___ ___ ___ ___ ___
2   44 54 25 7   19

C. A range of hills or mountains; elevated part of body (as backbone)

___ ___ ___ ___ ___
58 11 32 50 37

D. To get the alphabet started

___ ___ ___ ___ ___
16 40 36 9   31

E. Parish group; sacristy

___ ___ ___ ___ ___ ___
22 56 20 60 49 53

F. Stipulated; promised

___ ___ ___ ___ ___ ___
35 28 10 5   18 46

G. Standard; measure; average

___ ___ ___ ___
8   21 43 17

H. Ditchdigger's implement

___ ___ ___ ___ ___ ___
14 4   39 55 26 47

83

I. Condition causing
wheezing and
labored breathing

$\overline{48}$ $\overline{38}$ $\overline{13}$ $\overline{29}$ $\overline{1}$ $\overline{59}$

J. Reclaim; convert;
recover

$\overline{24}$ $\overline{23}$ $\overline{62}$ $\overline{42}$ $\overline{51}$ $\overline{6}$

K. A dog's sharp, shrill
bark

$\overline{3}$ $\overline{45}$ $\overline{52}$ $\overline{33}$

QUOTATION:

1i	2b	3k	4h	5f	6j

7b	8g	9d

10f	11c	12a	13i	14h

15a	16d	17g	18f	19b	20e

21g	22e	23j	24j	25b	26h	27a	28f	29i	30a	31d	32c

33k	34a	35f	36d	37c	38i

39h	40d	41a	42j	43g	44b	45k	46f

47h	48i	49e	50c	51j	52k	53e

54b	55h	56e	57a	58c	59i	60e	61a	62j

CLUES:

A. Lump, sizable quantity

—— —— —— —— ——
45 36 48 11 21

B. Removal, eviction, expulsion

—— —— —— —— —— ——
33 23 38 49 26 6

C. "The Rape of the ————," poem by Alexander Pope (1714)

—— —— —— ——
28 44 8 17

D. Choice, alternative

—— —— —— —— —— ——
19 27 9 37 47 43

E. Leopold von ————, (1795–1886), German historian, *History of the Popes* (1840)

—— —— —— —— ——
16 31 18 46 7

F. German masterpiece, written in two parts (1770 and 1831)

—— —— —— —— ——
34 2 13 32 24

G. Representation, likeness; popular conception

—— —— —— —— ——
29 1 5 12 40

85

H. Earth goddess who appears in *Das Rheingold* and *Siegfried*

$\overline{}_{4}$ $\overline{}_{25}$ $\overline{}_{41}$ $\overline{}_{15}$

I. Lock, fasten; attach oneself

$\overline{}_{14}$ $\overline{}_{10}$ $\overline{}_{35}$ $\overline{}_{20}$ $\overline{}_{39}$

J. Moor; deprive of pay

$\overline{}_{3}$ $\overline{}_{22}$ $\overline{}_{30}$ $\overline{}_{42}$

QUOTATION:

1g	2f	3j	4h

5g

6b	7e	8c	9d	10i	11a	12g	13f	14i	15h	16e

17c	18e	19d	20i	21a	22j	23b	24f

25h	26b	27d	28c	29g	30j	31e	32f

33b	34f

35i	36a	37d	38b

39i	40g	41h

42j	43d	44c	45a	46e

47d	48a	49b

COUPLET-CROSTIC #9

CLUES:

A. Cries of approbation

<u>　</u> <u>　</u> <u>　</u> <u>　</u> <u>　</u> <u>　</u>
27　20　38　14　33　61

B. One who brings out or causes to appear

<u>　</u> <u>　</u> <u>　</u> <u>　</u> <u>　</u> <u>　</u>
13　22　46　26　2　37

C. Winter Olympic sport

<u>　</u> <u>　</u> <u>　</u> <u>　</u>
10　19　1　29

D. In *Hamlet,* the vengeful brother

<u>　</u> <u>　</u> <u>　</u> <u>　</u> <u>　</u> <u>　</u> <u>　</u>
5　31　21　7　23　45　54

E. State bordering on the Arabian sea, capital Aden

<u>　</u> <u>　</u> <u>　</u> <u>　</u> <u>　</u>
60　6　50　8　34

F. Smooth woolen yarn used in fabrics

<u>　</u> <u>　</u> <u>　</u> <u>　</u> <u>　</u> <u>　</u> <u>　</u>
63　25　44　12　4　35　18

G. Vulgar, base; plebian

<u>　</u> <u>　</u> <u>　</u> <u>　</u> <u>　</u> <u>　</u> <u>　</u>
52　36　17　62　55　32　15

H. Sharp-pointed, two-edged surgical instrument

<u>　</u> <u>　</u> <u>　</u> <u>　</u> <u>　</u> <u>　</u>
28　51　39　42　16　59

I. In *Macbeth*, the
first victim

$\overline{40}\ \overline{58}\ \overline{3}\ \overline{9}\ \overline{41}\ \overline{53}$

J. Guarantee, make
certain

$\overline{49}\ \overline{64}\ \overline{47}\ \overline{11}\ \overline{24}\ \overline{56}$

K. Darn, curses!

$\overline{48}\ \overline{57}\ \overline{43}\ \overline{30}$

QUOTATION:

1c	2b	3i	4f	5d	6e			

7d	8e	9i	10c	11j	12f	13b	14a	15g

16h	17g	18f	19c	20a	21d	22b		

23d	24j	25f	26b	27a	28h	29c	30k	

31d	32g	33a	34e	35f				

36g	37b	38a	39h	40i			

41i	42h	43k	44f	45d	46b	47j	

48k	49j	50e	51h	52g	53i	54d	

55g	56j	57k	58i	59h	60e	61a	

62g	63f	64j					

COUPLET-CROSTIC #10

CLUES:

A. Relative by marriage

‾‾ ‾‾ ‾‾ ‾‾ ‾‾
40 14 34 22 25

B. Brain, noodle (slang)

‾‾ ‾‾ ‾‾ ‾‾ ‾‾ ‾‾
8 37 15 42 16 30

C. Eugene ——— (1855–1926), American Socialist

‾‾ ‾‾ ‾‾ ‾‾
9 44 5 24

D. Highest, greatest; best of one's abilities

‾‾ ‾‾ ‾‾ ‾‾ ‾‾ ‾‾
7 39 46 2 10 20

E. Throttle

‾‾ ‾‾ ‾‾ ‾‾ ‾‾ ‾‾ ‾‾ ‾‾
19 43 36 45 28 31 33 13

F. New York City political machine

‾‾ ‾‾ ‾‾ ‾‾ ‾‾ ‾‾ ‾‾
35 26 11 23 4 17 3

G. Assemble again; rebut

‾‾ ‾‾ ‾‾ ‾‾ ‾‾ ‾‾
27 21 1 6 29 41

H. Irish writer, won
Nobel Prize for
Literature in 1923

‾‾ ‾‾ ‾‾ ‾‾ ‾‾
12 18 32 38 47

QUOTATION:

‾‾ ‾‾ ‾‾
1g 2d 3f

‾‾ ‾‾ ‾‾ ‾‾ ‾‾ ‾‾ ‾‾
4f 5c 6g 7d 8b 9c 10d

‾‾ ‾‾
11f 12h

‾‾ ‾‾ ‾‾ ‾‾ ‾‾ ‾‾
13e 14a 15b 16b 17f 18h

‾‾ ‾‾ ‾‾ ‾‾ ‾‾ ‾‾
19e 20d 21g 22a 23f 24c

‾‾ ‾‾ ‾‾ ‾‾ ‾‾ ‾‾ ‾‾
25a 26f 27g 28e 29g 30b 31e

‾‾ ‾‾ ‾‾
32h 33e 34a

‾‾ ‾‾ ‾‾ ‾‾ ‾‾ ‾‾ ‾‾ ‾‾
35f 36e 37b 38h 39d 40a 41g 42b

‾‾ ‾‾ ‾‾ ‾‾ ‾‾
43e 44c 45e 46d 47h

♦ COUPLET-CROSTIC #11 ♦

CLUES:

A. "Queen of the
————," character
in Mozart's *The
Magic Flute*

__ __ __ __ __
29 35 17 42 19

B. Relating to horses

__ __ __ __ __ __
2 33 56 28 50 11

C. Cried

__ __ __ __
58 54 6 44

D. Skater's jump

__ __ __ __
40 12 72 38

E. French
Impressionist (1832–
1883), *Dejeuner sur
l'herbe*

__ __ __ __ __
5 15 41 32 53

F. Séance for persons
in Clues E and I

__ __ __ __ __ __ __
67 69 36 45 21 57 30

G. Herb of the
mustard family, with
thick root eaten as
vegetable

__ __ __ __ __ __
68 34 9 64 48 1

H. Amount, degree, space

$\overline{4}$ $\overline{24}$ $\overline{61}$ $\overline{18}$ $\overline{16}$ $\overline{52}$

I. French Impressionist (1840–1919), *Moulin de la Galette*

$\overline{3}$ $\overline{23}$ $\overline{47}$ $\overline{8}$ $\overline{60}$ $\overline{31}$

J. Dump, stand up, jilt

$\overline{55}$ $\overline{65}$ $\overline{62}$ $\overline{26}$ $\overline{20}$

K. Olympian, sportsman

$\overline{43}$ $\overline{7}$ $\overline{14}$ $\overline{71}$ $\overline{63}$ $\overline{27}$ $\overline{51}$

L. American Impressionist (1844–1926), *Cup of Tea, Reading Le Figaro* (full name)

$\overline{39}$ $\overline{25}$ $\overline{59}$ $\overline{10}$ $\overline{13}$ $\overline{37}$ $\overline{22}$ $\overline{49}$ $\overline{46}$ $\overline{66}$ $\overline{70}$

QUOTATION:

1g	2b	3i	4h	5e	6c	7k	8i	9g	10l

11b	12d	13l	14k	15e	16h	17a	18h

19a	20j	21f	22l

23i	24h	25l	26j	27k	28b	29a	30f

31i	32e	33b	34g	35a	36f	37l	38d

39l 40d 41e 42a 43k 44c 45f 46l 47i

48g 49l

50b 51k 52h 53e 54c 55j

56b 57f 58c 59l 60i 61h 62j 63k 64g

65j 66l 67f

68g 69f 70l 71k 72d

COUPLET-CROSTIC #12

CLUES:

A. Composer of "Titan"
and "Resurrection"
symphonies

—— —— —— —— —— ——
26 12 48 46   2 25

B. Jimmy Carter's
Ambassador to the
United Nations

—— —— —— —— ——
45 49 27   1   8

C. "The ——— of Young
Werther"

—— —— —— —— —— —— ——
 9 39 28 17   5   3 19

D. English dessert

—— —— —— —— —— ——
21 31   6 14 37 51

E. A play in football; an
evasive trick

—— —— —— —— —— ——
24   7 42 33 40 20

F. Shingler

—— —— —— —— —— ——
38 22 10 13 30 52

G. A simple poem or
musical composition
with a pastoral or
romantic theme (alt.
sp.)

—— —— —— ——
16 29 47 36

H. Shakespearean actor, also appeared on TV's *Bewitched*

$\overline{32}$ $\overline{23}$ $\overline{15}$ $\overline{11}$ $\overline{43}$

I. Toiling, laboring

$\overline{34}$ $\overline{44}$ $\overline{35}$ $\overline{50}$ $\overline{18}$ $\overline{41}$ $\overline{4}$

QUOTATION:

1b	2a	3c

4i	5c	6d	7e	8b	9c	10f	11h

12a	13f	14d	15h	16g	17c

18i	19c	20e	21d

22f	23h	24e	25a

26a	27b	28c	29g	30f	31d	32h	33e	34i

35i	36g	37d

38f	39c	40e	41i	42e

43h	44i	45b	46a	47g

48a	49b	50i	51d	52f

95

CLUES:

A. Sifter, strainer

‾41‾ ‾27‾ ‾5‾ ‾38‾ ‾14‾

B. Rectitude, integrity, uprightness

‾45‾ ‾9‾ ‾31‾ ‾1‾ ‾18‾ ‾12‾ ‾20‾

C. Deathly pale

‾8‾ ‾47‾ ‾13‾ ‾16‾ ‾28‾

D. Located under the earth's surface (poetical)

‾6‾ ‾37‾ ‾42‾ ‾33‾ ‾23‾ ‾25‾

E. Visitors, company

‾10‾ ‾26‾ ‾2‾ ‾36‾ ‾32‾ ‾24‾

F. Diminish, decrease

‾7‾ ‾46‾ ‾3‾ ‾15‾ ‾29‾ ‾40‾

G. Breathe one's last

‾11‾ ‾19‾ ‾22‾ ‾44‾ ‾35‾ ‾39‾

H. "Unsex me here, and fill me from the crown to the toe top-full of _____ cruelty." (Lady Macbeth, Act I, sc. v)

$\overline{}$ $\overline{}$ $\overline{}$ $\overline{}$ $\overline{}$ $\overline{}$
30 21 43 34 17 4

QUOTATION:

$\overline{1b}$ $\overline{2e}$ $\overline{3f}$ $\overline{4h}$

$\overline{5a}$ $\overline{6d}$ $\overline{7f}$ $\overline{8c}$ $\overline{9b}$ $\overline{10e}$ $\overline{11g}$

$\overline{12b}$ $\overline{13c}$ $\overline{14a}$ $\overline{15f}$ $\overline{16c}$

$\overline{17h}$ $\overline{18b}$ $\overline{19g}$

$\overline{20b}$ $\overline{21h}$ $\overline{22g}$ $\overline{23d}$ $\overline{24e}$

$\overline{25d}$ $\overline{26e}$ $\overline{27a}$ $\overline{28c}$ $\overline{29f}$ $\overline{30h}$

$\overline{31b}$ $\overline{32e}$ $\overline{33d}$ $\overline{34h}$ $\overline{35g}$

$\overline{36e}$ $\overline{37d}$ $\overline{38a}$ $\overline{39g}$ $\overline{40f}$

$\overline{41a}$ $\overline{42d}$ $\overline{43h}$ $\overline{44g}$ $\overline{45b}$ $\overline{46f}$ $\overline{47c}$

CLUES:

A. American film
director, *Stop
Making Sense,
Something Wild*

___ ___ ___ ___ ___
9 28 10 51 5

B. Employ

___ ___ ___
11 45 50

C. French
choreographer,
founder *Ballet of
the XXth Century*

___ ___ ___ ___ ___ ___
13 18 1 7 27 48

D. Upper part of the
trachea, containing
the vocal cords

___ ___ ___ ___ ___ ___
14 29 6 37 19 47

E. River in southern
Asia, flowing from
Tibet through
Pakistan to the
Arabian Sea

___ ___ ___ ___ ___
15 33 20 41 24

F. Birgit ———,
Swedish Wagnerian
soprano

—— —— —— —— —— —— ——
16 32 21 43 25 38 36

G. Test; critical study

—— —— —— —— —— ——
46 34 2 12 44 8

H. American composer
of operettas, *The
Student Prince,
Desert Song*

—— —— —— —— —— —— ——
49 35 30 4 22 42 17

I. Melodic phrase
forming the basis of
a composition or
movement

—— —— —— —— —— —— ——
23 39 3 31 52 40 26

QUOTATION:

—— —— —— —— —— ——
1c 2g 3i 4h 5a 6d

—— —— ——
7c 8g 9a

—— —— —— —— —— —— —— ——
10a 11b 12g 13c 14d 15e 16f 17h

—— —— —— —— —— —— ——
18c 19d 20e 21f 22h 23i 24e

—— —— —— —— —— ——
25f 26i 27c 28a 29d 30h

—— —— —— ——
31i 32f 33e 34g

—— ——
35h 36f

99

37d	38f	39i			
40i	41e	42h	43f	44g	45b

46g	47d	48c	49h	50b	51a	52i

COUPLET-CROSTIC #15

CLUES:

A. Conductor Seiji
____

— — — — —
18 48 43 24 29

B. Literature, learning

— — — — — — —
28 45 8 37 13 14 36

C. City northeast of
Manhattan on the
Hudson

— — — — — — —
6 49 39 21 32 41 17

D. Pierre ____-France,
French premier
(1954–1955)

— — — — — —
1 15 25 44 11 33

E. Leopard, cougar

— — — — — — —
27 16 22 12 4 51 46

F. Discernment,
understanding

— — — — — — —
38 19 30 2 3 9 40

G. The ____ Jungle,
early Marilyn
Monroe film

— — — — — — —
7 47 34 31 35 10 5

H. Forward ends of
airplanes

$\overline{50}$ $\overline{23}$ $\overline{26}$ $\overline{42}$ $\overline{20}$

QUOTATION:

$\overline{1d}$ $\overline{2f}$ $\overline{3f}$ $\overline{4e}$ $\overline{5g}$ $\overline{6c}$

$\overline{7g}$ $\overline{8b}$ $\overline{9f}$ $\overline{10g}$ $\overline{11d}$ $\overline{12e}$ $\overline{13b}$

$\overline{14b}$ $\overline{15d}$ $\overline{16e}$ $\overline{17c}$ $\overline{18a}$ $\overline{19f}$ $\overline{20h}$

$\overline{21c}$ $\overline{22e}$ $\overline{23h}$ $\overline{24a}$ $\overline{25d}$

$\overline{26h}$ $\overline{27e}$ $\overline{28b}$ $\overline{29a}$ $\overline{30f}$ $\overline{31g}$ $\overline{32c}$ $\overline{33d}$

$\overline{34g}$ $\overline{35g}$ $\overline{36b}$ $\overline{37b}$

$\overline{38f}$ $\overline{39c}$

$\overline{40f}$ $\overline{41c}$ $\overline{42h}$ $\overline{43a}$ $\overline{44d}$ $\overline{45b}$ $\overline{46e}$ $\overline{47g}$

$\overline{48a}$ $\overline{49c}$ $\overline{50h}$ $\overline{51e}$

◆ COUPLET-CROSTIC #16 ◆

CLUES:

A. Hetty ——— (1834–
1916), eccentric
financier, known as
"Witch of Wall
Street"

—— —— —— —— ——
26   4   39 21 13

B. Strata

—— —— —— —— —— ——
18 27 37   3   6 44

C. Bay, recess in the
shore; creek

—— —— —— —— ——
30   8 36 25 15

D. Slowing of blood
circulation;
equilibrium

—— —— —— —— —— ——
32 28 40 22   2 31

E. Thin, fine, delicate;
indirect

—— —— —— —— —— ——
9   33 17 23 24 46

F. Islands in the North
Atlantic, 800 miles
west of Portugal

—— —— —— —— —— ——
10 20 42 34 19 47

103

G. Neat, trim

$\overline{11}$ $\overline{16}$ $\overline{45}$ $\overline{43}$ $\overline{5}$

H. Tin-glazed Dutch earthenware, often in blue and white

$\overline{12}$ $\overline{35}$ $\overline{41}$ $\overline{1}$ $\overline{48}$

I. Unsweetened Greek liqueur

$\overline{14}$ $\overline{7}$ $\overline{38}$ $\overline{29}$

QUOTATION:

1h	2d	3b	4a	5g		

6b	7i	8c	9e

10f	11g	12h

13a	14i	15c	16g	17e	18b	19f

20f	21a	22d	23e

24e	25c	26a	27b	28d	29i

30c	31d

32d	33e	34f	35h	36c	37b

38i	39a	40d	41h	42f	43g	44b

45g	46e	47f	48h

◆ # COUPLET-CROSTIC #17 ◆

CLUES:

A. Medieval;
barbarous; macabre
‾‾ ‾‾ ‾‾ ‾‾ ‾‾ ‾‾
18 39 51 3 32 60

B. Spacious
‾‾ ‾‾ ‾‾ ‾‾ ‾‾
10 7 62 19 46

C. U.S. athlete, track
and field, won 4
gold medals in 1936
Olympics
‾‾ ‾‾ ‾‾ ‾‾ ‾‾
4 49 43 17 34

D. Lehar's *The Merry*
‾‾‾‾‾
‾‾ ‾‾ ‾‾ ‾‾ ‾‾
40 61 6 48 14

E. Lettering
‾‾ ‾‾ ‾‾ ‾‾
52 36 58 9

F. District in Los
Angeles
‾‾ ‾‾ ‾‾ ‾‾ ‾‾ ‾‾ ‾‾ ‾‾ ‾‾
47 13 5 38 56 24 44 2 15

G. Small stream, brook
‾‾ ‾‾ ‾‾ ‾‾ ‾‾ ‾‾ ‾‾
45 26 8 63 55 33 1

H. Semicircular part of
basilica
‾‾ ‾‾ ‾‾ ‾‾
23 29 64 53

105

I. Roman historian (circa A.D. 56–120), *Historiae, Dialogue on Orators*

$\overline{27}$ $\overline{37}$ $\overline{31}$ $\overline{16}$ $\overline{41}$ $\overline{50}$ $\overline{21}$

J. Card game in which three tricks win a hand

$\overline{59}$ $\overline{20}$ $\overline{11}$ $\overline{42}$ $\overline{54}$ $\overline{30}$

K. Native intelligence, savvy

$\overline{28}$ $\overline{35}$ $\overline{25}$ $\overline{12}$ $\overline{22}$ $\overline{57}$

QUOTATION:

$\overline{1g}$ $\overline{2f}$

$\overline{3a}$ $\overline{4c}$ $\overline{5f}$ $\overline{6d}$

$\overline{7b}$ $\overline{8g}$ $\overline{9e}$ $\overline{10b}$ $\overline{11j}$ $\overline{12k}$ $\overline{13f}$ $\overline{14d}$ $\overline{15f}$ $\overline{16i}$ $\overline{17c}$ $\overline{18a}$

$\overline{19b}$ $\overline{20j}$ $\overline{21i}$ $\overline{22k}$

$\overline{23h}$ $\overline{24f}$ $\overline{25k}$ $\overline{26g}$ $\overline{27i}$

$\overline{28k}$ $\overline{29h}$ $\overline{30j}$ $\overline{31i}$ $\overline{32a}$ $\overline{33g}$ $\overline{34c}$

$\overline{35k}$ $\overline{36e}$

$\overline{37i}$

$\overline{38f}$ $\overline{39a}$ $\overline{40d}$

106

41i	42j	43c	44f	45g	46b

47f	48d	49c

50i	51a	52e	53h	54j	55g	56f

57k	58e	59j	60a	61d	62b	63g	64h

CLUES:

A. In the middle of

—— —— —— ——
22 5 15 31

B. Architectural style;
woman's haircut

—— —— —— —— —— —— ——
45 17 12 30 4 23 43

C. Mountain range
between
Czechoslovakia and
Poland

—— —— —— —— —— —— ——
13 2 37 26 38 49 20

D. City in northern
Utah

—— —— —— —— ——
9 16 3 27 44

E. '———, *Mother,*
play by Marsha
Norman

—— —— —— —— ——
36 32 21 11 42

F. "Leaving On ———
Plane," song by
Peter, Paul, and
Mary (2 wds.)

—— —— —— ——
47 1 29 18

G. Dorothy Sayers
novel, *The ——*
Tailors

$\overline{14}$ $\overline{39}$ $\overline{33}$ $\overline{6}$

H. Small slit;
loophole; narrow
beam of light

$\overline{46}$ $\overline{41}$ $\overline{19}$ $\overline{7}$ $\overline{25}$

I. Aubergine

$\overline{24}$ $\overline{34}$ $\overline{40}$ $\overline{28}$ $\overline{48}$ $\overline{35}$ $\overline{10}$ $\overline{8}$

QUOTATION:

1f	2c	3d	4b	5a	6g	7h	8i

9d	10i

11e	12b	13c

14g	15a	16d	17b	18f	19h	20c	21e	22a	23b	24i

25h	26c	27d	28i

29f	30b	31a	32e	33g	34i

35i	36e	37c

38c	39g	40i	41h	42e	43b	44d

45b	46h	47f	48i	49c

PALINDROMES

I must admit I've enjoyed digging into the background of all the word games I've included in *Names Games*. Tony Augarde's book *The Oxford Guide to Word Games* contains a wealth of material—I can't recommend it highly enough. When I decided I needed to dig deeper, I merely looked up anagrams, acrostics, and palindromes in the Oxford English Dictionary. The definitions contained dozens of citations to old obscure books, many of which I was able to request in the Boston Public Library. I remember a feeling of amazement when a librarian brought to my table a dusty old tome—it was an edition of Chambers's Encyclopaedia from the 1800s—not on microfilm, but the real book. I hardly thought they let you put your hands on these fading treasures anymore. In it I found that loving couplet of Cotton Mather's on anagrams I mentioned earlier. But I've also had some unlikely sources of information—my cousin Clark Thomson, for one.

Clark was down on Cape Cod this summer when I was visiting our grandmother in Chatham. One day in the car he told one of the best palindrome stories I've ever heard. It seems that several years earlier he and a group of college chums were enjoying themselves at a local tavern. I don't know how the subject came up, but at one point Clark started asking "What do you call those phrases that read the same backward and forward? The word's on the tip of my tongue." Some of his friends knew vaguely what he was talking about, but no one could supply the answer. Clark challenged them to try harder and even offered a free beer to the genius who could retrieve the answer. Suddenly, across the room, a slightly tight patron at the bar leaned in their direction and started calling out, "Race car, race car." Huh? Clark's group wondered. "Race car," he chanted, indicating he was trying to shed some light on Clark's mystery. "No, I know it's not called a 'race car,'" Clark called back, wishing by now that he'd never brought up the subject. Still the guy came back with "race car."

Well, you've probably realized by now that "race car" is merely another example of a palindrome, a word or phrase that reads the same backward and forward. I had never come across it in my various word books or ancient encyclopedias, and I must say it is remarkable for its brevity. So I offer a toast to this anonymous hanger-on.

Most people know a few of the more famous palindromes: "Madam, I'm Adam" and "Able was I ere I saw Elba" (supposedly uttered by Napoleon during his first banishment). And of course, there is one other famous palindrome, by common agreement the finest we have: A man, A plan, A canal—Panama! Attributed to the Englishman Leigh Mercer, this majestic phrase stands as a shrine to all lovers of palindromes. It contains all that is best in this form: economy of words, ringing assonance, a grand build-up to that final stirring word, and, above all, blessed lucidity. (My cousin Clark added his own fine compliment when he remarked to me, "And you know, it doesn't sound like a palindrome.")

Palindromes can get fairly convoluted and obscure as the writer tries to line up the letters symmetrically. Sometimes the results verge on the surrealistic. But as we've seen with anagrams, and as we will soon discover in the "pangram" challenge, it is much better to strive for clarity, as much as these complicated forms permit.

My palindromes almost didn't make it into this book. They were not in puzzle form in the beginning, and neither I nor the resourceful editors at Dell saw a way to make them work as puzzles. I had resigned myself to leaving the palindromes out of the book entirely until, just a few days before I was to submit the final manuscript, the puzzle format for the palindrome came to me. You'll now have the chance to recreate some of my palindromes, but before you get started we will have to spend a little time analyzing the structure of the palindrome.

BACKGROUND

As you know, palindromes are words or phrases that read the same backward and forward. This means that at its exact midpoint the palindrome will "pivot" on a letter and work its way to the end as a mirror image of the beginning half. So a palindrome is divided into two equal parts, with a pivot letter right in the middle. A palindrome of, let's say, fifteen letters will have two "halves" of seven letters each, with the pivot occurring as the eighth letter in the phrase ($7 + 1 + 7 = 15$ letters).

From what I've just described, you might assume that palindromes always contain an odd number of letters (two halves of equal letters, plus the pivot letter). This structure holds true most of the time, but occasionally a palindrome can have an even number of letters. I will point them out in the text to follow. I am utterly at a loss to explain these bizarre even-letter palindromes. They do read the same backward and forward, so they are legitimate palindromes. I just can't understand why they don't have an odd number of letters. If anyone can shed light on this matter I'd be very grateful. But for the moment let's return to the palindromes with an odd total of letters.

The pivot letter is the palindrome's signpost, alerting you that all the letters to its right are repeated, in reverse order, to its left. Because of the wonders of this pivot letter, and because I have tried to write palindromes with "sense" in mind, the palindromes can be turned into puzzles, which leads us to the following:

INSTRUCTIONS

- You are asked to recreate the palindromes that follow, whose words are indicated by a series of numbered dashes. The pivot letter in the middle is clearly indicated by a capital *P*. Each dash corresponds to a letter in the palindrome. They are grouped together to indicate word length, and punctuation has been inserted. The dashes are numbered in a peculiar way to help you in the final stages. Starting from the left, they rise consecutively from number 1 until they hit the pivot letter, then they descend to number 1 to the right of the pivot letter. These numbers will help you remember the mirror image of the palindrome. If dash number 3 on the left should be the letter *S*, dash number 3 on the right will also have to be an *S*.
- To get started, you must first unscramble a series of jumbled letters to form one of the palindrome words. The letter scramble appears directly under the dashes corresponding to the palindrome word you are to make. When you have unscrambled the letters into a word, place them in the dashes directly above. This is probably the most difficult step of the operation.
- Next, locate the pivot letter, which should occur near the end or the beginning of your unscrambled word. You now start filling in the dashes to the immediate right or left of the pivot letter by reversing those letters in your unscrambled word. Use the numbers below the dashes as your guide. You should start to see palindrome words forming.
- The longer palindromes present a special problem, so you will need some extra help to fill in the dashes beyond the range of the pivot point. In these cases I have chosen one of two options: 1) I have filled in one or two letters in their respective left/right positions, and you must use your powers of intuition to fill in the words. 2) I present another letter scramble for one of the other palindrome words. When you have unscrambled this word you will be able to fill in the corresponding letters on the other side of the

116

pivot point. At all times, remember the mirror-image quality of the palindrome.

- Finally, I give you a sense of what the palindrome is all about or which famous person might have said it. This clue should keep you on track as you attempt to form words in the dashes, and it may even help you as you unscramble the first group of letters into a meaningful word.

- As in the riddlegram section, I have included a few freebies—some of my longer palindromes would be too cumbersome to solve as puzzles—but I wanted you to have a chance to see them.

A famous palindrome followed by an appropriate palindrome response:

He: MADAM, I'M ADAM
She: *NAME IS EVESIE, MAN*

Two famous palindromes, each followed by an appropriate anagram.

ABLE WAS I ERE I SAW ELBA

O, NOT A NAPPER ON ELBA (Napoleon Bonaparte)

A MAN, A PLAN, A CANAL—PANAMA

RETOTE SOD OVER HOLE (Theodore Roosevelt)

Palindromes some previously encountered subjects might have said:

1. $\underline{}\ \underline{}\ \underline{}\ \underline{}\ \underline{\textbf{P}}\quad \underline{}\ \underline{}\ \underline{}\ \underline{}$

    1 2 3 4 **P**   4 3 2 1

T F I S F

                    A comment Yves Saint Laurent might make

2. ___ ___ ___ ___ ___ **P** , ___ ___ ___ ___ ___ ?

    1 2 3 4 5 **P**   5 4   3 2 1

W O B R O R

                    A question T. S. Eliot might ask himself

3. ___ ' ___ ___ ___ ___ ___ **P** 6 ___ ___ ___ ___ ___

    1   2   3 4 5 6 **P** 6   5 4 3 2 1

    E E R V E R

                    An admission of Maria "Avid Diva" Callas

4. $\overline{}\ \overline{}\ \overline{}\quad \overline{}\ \overline{}\ \underline{\textbf{P}}\ ,\quad \overline{}\quad \overline{}\ \overline{}\ \overline{}\ \overline{}$
    1 2 3   4 5 **P**   5   4 3 2 1

N W O K

Something Oedipus Rex's mother might say

RETRACT, CARTER!

   —Ronald Reagan

LEVER, LEVEL, REVEL

   —Donald Trump

REDIVIDE DIVIDER

   —Mies van der Rohe

LOOPS POP SPOOL

   —Couplet-Crostic #13

Palindromes some miscellaneous people might have said:

5. $\underline{}\ \underline{}\ \underline{}\ \underline{}\ \underline{}\ \underline{}\ \underline{}\ \underline{}\ \ \underline{}\ \underline{}\ \underline{}\ \underline{}\ ,\ \ \underline{}\ \underline{}\ \underline{}\ \ \underline{}\ \underline{}$

  1 2 3 4 5 6 7 8 **P** 8 7 6 , 5 4 3 2 1

T E I N R I S S

Something John Calvin might say to his congregation

LIVE DEMON GNOME DEVIL

   —Mephistopheles

GIRDLE HELD RIG

   —Mae West

6. $\underline{}\ \underline{}\ \underline{}\ \underline{}\ \underline{}\ \underline{}\ \ \underline{}\ \underline{}\ \underline{}\ \underline{}\ \ \underline{}\ \underline{}\ \underline{}$

  1 2 3 4 5 6 **P** 6 5 4 3 2 1

R E T D A S

A description of Bernard Berenson

7. _ _ _ _ _ _ _ _ _ _ _ _ _
  1 2 3 4 5 6 **P** 6 5 4 3 2 1

O R I D O B N

A confession of Modest Mussorgsky

(Note: Letter scramble is a proper name.)

8. D _ A _ , _ _ _ _ _ _ _ ... _ _ _
  1 2 3 4   5 6 7 8 9 10 11 **P** 11 10

I T A M N E A

_ _ _ _ _ _ A _ D
9 8 7 6 5 4 3 2 1

A cry of Vincent Van Gogh

DROLL LORD

—P. G. Wodehouse

DIARY RAID

—Samuel Pepys

TUG AT A GUT

—Jane Fonda

9. $\underset{1}{\_}\,\underset{2}{\_}\,\underset{3}{B}\quad\underset{4}{\_}\,\underset{5}{\_}\,\underset{6}{\_}\,\underset{7}{\_}\,\underset{8}{\_}\,\underset{9}{\_}$:

U X T L E S

" $\underset{10}{\_}\,\underset{\underline{P}}{\_}\,\underset{10}{\_}\,\underset{9}{\_}\,\underset{8}{\_}$, $\underset{7}{\_}\,\underset{6}{\_}\,\underset{5}{\_}\,\underset{4}{\_}\,\underset{3}{B}\,\underset{2}{\_}\,\underset{1}{\_}$!"

Palindrome for a Sloane Ranger

10. $\underset{1}{\_}\,\underset{2}{\_}\quad\underset{3}{\_}\,\underset{4}{\_}\,\underset{5}{\_}\,\underset{6}{\_}\quad\underset{\underline{P}}{\_}\,\underset{6}{\_}\quad\underset{5}{\_}\,\underset{4}{\_}\,\underset{3}{\_}\,\underset{2}{\_}\,\underset{1}{\_}$

I N D A A

Proclamation of Prince Charles

122

11. _ _ _ _ _ , _ _ _ _ _ _ !
   1 2 3 4 5   P 5 4 3 2 1

   E L S W A

A response to Palindrome #10

(Note: Scramble words for Palindromes #10 and #11 are proper names.)

12. _ _ _ _ _ _ _ _ _ _ _ _ _
   1 2 3 4 5 6   7 8 9 10 P   10

   P I R E D A   L O A T T

   _ _ _ _ _ _ _ _ _
   9 8 7 6 5 4 3 2 1

        P I R E D A

        Palindrome for a thoughtful child

(Caution: Letters 1→6 and, conversely, 6→1 yield two words that are mirror anagrams of one another. Also note the additional scramble word for letters 7→P.)

13. _ _ _ _ _ _ _ _   _ _ _   _ _   _   _ _ _
    1 2 3 4 5 6 7 8   **P** 8 7   6 5   4   3 2 1

E T I N D I F E

Palindrome for a computer programmer

14. _ _ _ _ , _ _ _ _L_ _ _ _ _ _
    1 2 3 4   5 6 7   8 9 10 11   12 13

I N S O M E T S E

_ _ _ _ ... _ _ _ _ _ _ _ _ _
14 15 16 17   **P** 17 16 15 14 13 12 11 10

_L_ _ _' _ _ _ _ _
 9 8 7   6   5 4 3 2 1

Palindrome for a flautist

(Clues: Words 1→4 and 14→17 are the same. Also note the
apostrophe between 6→5.)

*ME GONE! VIOLIN IN A GAP. STRAD ARTS . . . PAGANINI
. . . LO, I'VE NO GEM*

—The "lost fiddle" palindrome

124

Palindromes for a magazine staff:

STORY ROTS

   —Fiction editor

KNITS STINK

   —Fashion editor

15. $\underline{}\ \underline{}\ \underline{}\ \underline{}$, $\underline{}\ \underline{}\ \underline{}\ \underline{\textbf{P}}$ $\underline{}\ \underline{}\ \underline{}\ \underline{}\ \underline{}\ \underline{}\ \underline{}$
   1   2   3   4   5   6   7   **P**   7   6   5   4   3   2   1

E   C   M   I   S   A   N

Palindrome for the film editor

16. $\underline{}\ \underline{}\ \underline{\textbf{D}}\ \underline{}$ $\underline{}\ \underline{}\ \underline{}\ \underline{}$ $\underline{}\ \underline{\textbf{P}}\ \underline{}\ \underline{}\ \underline{}\ \underline{}\ \underline{}\ \underline{}$
   1   2   3   4   5   6   7   8   9   **P**   9   8   7   6   5   4

L   E   P   P   I   N   I   E

$\underline{\textbf{D}}\ \underline{}\ \underline{}$
 3   2   1

Palindrome for the Egyptian oil minister

125

17.

$\frac{}{1}\ \frac{}{2}\ \frac{}{3}\ \frac{}{4}\ \frac{}{5}\ \frac{}{6}\quad \frac{}{7}\ \frac{}{8}\ \frac{}{9}\ \frac{}{10}\ \underline{\textbf{P}}$

W E R D A R   R Y T A S

$\frac{}{10}\ \frac{}{9}\ \frac{}{8}\ \frac{}{7}\quad \frac{}{6}\ \frac{}{5}\ \frac{}{4}\ \frac{}{3}\ \frac{}{2}\ \frac{}{1}$

W E R D A R

Palindrome for the National Endowment for the Arts

(Caution: Words 1→6 and 6→1 are mirror image anagrams of one another. Also note the additional word scramble for letters 7→P.)

18.

$\frac{}{1}\ \frac{}{2}\ \frac{}{3}\ \frac{}{4}\ \frac{}{5}\ \underline{\textbf{P}}$, $\frac{}{5}$ ' $\frac{}{4}\quad \frac{}{3}\ \frac{}{2}\ \frac{}{1}$!

T I D M A M

An all-purpose expression of disgust and anger

19. $\underset{1}{\_} \underset{2}{M} \underset{3}{\_} \underset{4}{\_} \underset{5}{\_} \quad \underset{6}{\_} \underset{7}{\_} \underset{8}{\_} \underset{9}{\_} \underset{10}{\_}$, $\underset{\mathbf{P}}{\_} \underset{10}{\_} \underset{9}{\_}$

$\underset{8}{\_} \underset{7}{\_} \underset{6}{\_} \underset{5}{\_} \underset{4}{\_} \quad \underset{3}{\_} \underset{2}{M} \underset{1}{\_}$

D E S T A

Palindrome for a snob (#1)

◆ INEXPLICABLE PALINDROMES ◆

Here are the palindromes with an even number of letters:

> *SLIP-UP, BOO-BOO . . . BOOB PUPILS!*
> —Palindrome for Mr. Chips

> *NO, IT IS OPPOSED, IS SIDE'S OPPOSITION*
> —Palindrome for the House of Commons

Here's an example of the "Able was I" style. Here the palindrome does not glide through the letters of different words; each word is a distinct unit of the palindrome, and each word is accompanied by a mirror image anagram of itself.

> *REGAL GULP DID PLUG LAGER*
> —The "royal warrant" palindrome

> *REVOLT, LOVER!*
> —Palindrome for a cuckold

WE DROOP, LATE PETAL—POOR DEW.
—"The "flower's lament" palindrome

NOW, SATRAP, S.O.S. I'M, ALAS, XERXES, EX-REX.
SALAMIS . . . O SPARTA'S WON!
—Palindrome on the Battle of Salamis

(Note: The Battle of Salamis [Sept. 28, 480 B.C.] was a crushing defeat for the Persian invaders of Greece, headed by King Xerxes. Themistocles, the leader of the Athenians, played a decisive role in repelling the Persian force. Nevertheless, Salamis marked a suitable revenge for the Spartans, who had valiantly defended themselves against Xerxes at the famous battle of Thermopylae, which had taken place earlier that spring.

I may be guilty of rewriting history here, but if it lets me use "Xerxes" in a palindrome, isn't it worth it?)

DRAWERS DO OFTEN. A MONET SAW SAGE DEGAS
WASTE NO MANET FOOD'S REWARD
—The *Dejeuner sur l'herbe* palindrome

STARE, MOST ARE ELITE. SPOT A TOP SET?
I LEER AT SOME RATS!
—Palindrome for a snob (#2)

PANGRAMS

There are zillions of possible combinations (403,290,000,000,000,000,000,000,000 to be exact) of the twenty-six letters of the English alphabet. Yet despite this abundance, it has proven exceedingly difficult to compose a complete sentence that uses all the letters of the alphabet just once. Such a twenty-six letter monster sentence is called a "pangram," and it represents the ultimate challenge for wordsmiths.

There are numerous examples of fine sentences of twenty-nine letters or more, but obviously these repeat a few letters of the alphabet. Consider this well-known example: "The quick brown fox jumps over a lazy dog." At thirty-three letters it's not a perfect pangram, but typing instructors swear by it.

Somewhere in the alphabet there must be a complete sentence of twenty-six letters, just waiting to be discovered. Why then has the quest for this elusive pangram proved as fruitless as the search for two words that rhyme with "orange" and "silver"?

For starters, potential pangrammatists come right up against scarce vowels and tough consonants. The English alphabet contains only five vowels (six when you count *Y* in its vowel form). This makes at best twenty consonants and only six vowels, out of which must be formed an intelligible sentence. When you consider some of the consonants you realize how difficult the task is: *J, V, X, Z, W, K.* Used infrequently in English, these must be combined with the easier consonants (*R, S, M, D,* etc.) and the few vowels.

Of all the consonants, however, *Q* is the toughest. Normally, *Q* must be followed by *U* and another vowel, thereby leaving only four vowels available for the remaining words in the pangram sentence. Solve this *Q* problem and you may well crack the pangram.

Most wordsmiths get around the *Q* problem by resorting to obscure, archaic words or words that have been borrowed from exotic languages. Technically this is permissible, as long as the words appear in a reputable dictionary. The problem with this approach is that the resulting pangrams need to be paraphrased or translated into modern English. Here are a few examples of these sorts of pangrams, with their necessary glosses:

CWM, FJORD-BANK GLYPHS VEXT QUIZ
("Carved figures on the bank of a fjord in a rounded valley irritated an eccentric person.")

VEXT CWM FLY ZING JABS KURD QOPH
("An annoyed fly in a valley, humming shrilly, pokes at the nineteenth letter of the Hebrew alphabet drawn by a Kurd.")

When I attempted a pangram, I decided I did not want to use Welsh words like "cwm." The dictionary may say they are words, but I say they are algebraic notations and I wanted none of them in my pangrams.

How then to proceed? How to solve the *Q* problem and still use modern, everyday English words?

I am happy to report that the answer came to me quickly, pretty darned quickly as a matter of fact. PDQ is an acronym, a kind of semiword formed by stringing together the first letters of the words "pretty darned quick." By starting with this acronym, I disposed of the *Q* and had all six vowels available for the rest of my pangram. With this PDQ device I was able to create three intelligible pangrams that I believe meet all the technical requirements.

Alas, some usage experts claim that acronyms are not valid words, that they are in fact nothing more than glorified abbreviations and therefore should not be allowed in pangrams. I think we can all agree that initials and abbreviations in pangrams constitute a form of cheating. Some anonymous person has tried to fob off this sentence as a pangram: J. Q. SCHWARTZ FLUNG D. V. PIKE MY BOX. Clearly this is a feeble attempt, as almost anyone can throw together initials of imaginary persons to form a sentence.

Abbreviations are slightly more respectable than initials, but still not quite the thing I'd like to see in pangrams. Abbreviations by definition are shorthand for words. They stand in for words but can never be considered bona fide words themselves. Pronunciation provides experimental verification. When you read "Mr." on the page, you don't pronounce it as "Mra" or "Murr," but as "Mister." Similarly with Dr., Mrs., etc. (How did you read "etc." to yourself?) Even with an abbreviation that can be easily pronounced as a word, such as "lat." (for "latitude"), I think most people still verbalize it as "latitude" in their heads.

But with acronyms one rises up another level toward full-fledged wordhood. Acronyms such as GNP, SOS, or NATO look at first glance like initials and abbreviations. Indeed, they are formed by the initial letters of a string of words and stand in as a convenient shorthand for the word string. However, many reputable dictionaries honor some acronyms as words unto themselves. Here's how I believe the process works:

Acronyms become deeply entrenched in the language, so much so that speakers often cannot recall the original word string. Take two common acronyms, "scuba" and "radar." How many people think of Self Contained Underwater Breathing Apparatus or RAdio Detecting And Ranging when they say or write scuba and radar? Even the most curmudgeonly pedant would have to admit that scuba and radar are now valid words.

Nonetheless, not all acronyms are words. Only when people in large numbers embrace an acronym does it become a word. Consider the case of "NIMBY." Toxic waste dumps and incinerators located near residential areas may start multiplying like fungi patches. But let's hope not, or this recently coined acronym for Not In My Back Yard may rise to the status of a bona fide word. For the moment, though, NIMBY is an acronym trapped in a way station, neither abbreviation nor word.

Although I've become very pro-acronym since starting pangrams, I recognize that when acronyms get out of hand the language suffers. They must be used sparingly. Unfortunately we live in an age when large bureaucracies, especially the military and the computer industry, delight in churning out ever newer acronyms. It's impossible to keep up with them. For acronyms to work at all they must be readily understood. But burden us with too many acronyms and the language is reduced to an unintelligible alphabet soup. If we don't watch out, we will initialize and abbreviate ourselves into illiteracy.

In the end, no final arbiter can decide whether or when abbreviations are appropriate. But I think we can accept the pronouncement of Mario Pei, the eminent language scholar, in his book *The Story of English:**

"The language of abbreviations, alphabetical and otherwise, seems to be with us for keeps. It need not preoccupy us overmuch. Judging from what has happened in the past, those abbreviations which strike the popular fancy will develop into fresh words. The others will shrivel and fall away, along with the objects or institutions for which they stand."

Let's look at the particular case of PDQ. Most people know that PDQ means "immediately" or "at once," even if they can't identify "pretty darned quick" as the source. Open any Yellow Pages and you're sure to find a "PDQ Print Shop" or "PDQ Bicycle Courier" service. Obviously these companies wouldn't receive many calls if customers were mystified by PDQ.

From *The Story of English* by Mario Pei (New York, J. B. Lippincott Co., 1952).

Several liberal-minded dictionaries have now accepted PDQ. Webster's Third defines it as an adverb and even grants it the highest honor an acronym can receive: a phonetic transcription (pē-dē-kyü). Here is further evidence that acronyms are something other than garden variety abbreviations, which are not phonetically transcribed. Several other dictionaries, including the Oxford Dictionary of American English, also list this Americanism.

Stuart Flexner, in his *I Hear America Talking,* dates PDQ to the late 1860s. Thus it is one of the oldest acronyms around. By contrast, most acronyms came into use after World War I. Also, since many acronyms are slang, they don't tend to last long in general usage. PDQ is a remarkable exception.

So as justification for PDQ I offer its long-standing use in the language. I believe it ranks with scuba and radar as acronyms that have become words. But there is even a better reason why PDQ should be given special consideration. Most acronyms are used as nouns. Occasionally you see them working as verbs: "Mayor Nimbied by Angry Townspeople" (headline of the future?). But PDQ is the only acronym I can think of, besides the frantic exhortation "ASAP," that is used as an adverb.

I also question whether it is in the best interests of wordplay to allow obscure, archaic words in pangrams while elevating noses at valid acronyms. Much as I am amused by the cwms and zings and glyphs one usually encounters in pangrams, I would like to try for words that are slightly more accessible.

So I'd like to offer you my series of three PDQ pangrams. Be warned, though, that they are not written in the most elegant prose. I do believe they are understandable, however, especially with the titles I have supplied. Note that the "Music Critic" and "Shotgun Wedding" pangrams both use the same words, only in different order. If you can accept "schmaltz vow" as a liberal metaphor for "wedding," then you should enjoy the "Shotgun Wedding" pangram. It's my personal favorite.

The "Glasnost" pangram I am not so sure about. Here I use two acronyms and am possibly guilty of stretching the rules just a little too far. But KGB is as much a word as PDQ, so if my analysis of the acronym is valid I should be allowed to offer you the "glasnost" pangram. I especially like it because of the link between "KGB" and "czar."

THE PDQ PANGRAMS

The "Glasnost" Pangram
(or what an American TV news producer might urge his correspondent to do):

WHY, JUST VEX KGB CZAR ON FILM—PDQ!

The "Music Critic's" Pangram
(headline to a review of a terrible concert):

VOW: FIX BY GUN SCHMALTZ JERK, PDQ!

THE "SHOTGUN WEDDING" PANGRAM

BY GUN JERK FIX SCHMALTZ VOW, PDQ!

◆

FAREWELL TO
THE READER

◆

You, Our Uncommon, Radiant Set.
Thanks, Readers—Unravel Letters, Yet!

SOLUTIONS

RIDDLEGRAMS

THE BIG BAD WOLF	**WHAT IF GOBBLED?**
BENEDICT ARNOLD	**IN REDCOAT BLEND**
DOLLEY MADISON	**ONE LADY SO MILD**
RONALD REAGAN	**DARN NEAR GOAL**
GEORGE BUSH	**BUGS GO HERE**
OLIVER L. NORTH	**ROLL IN TV HERO**
DANIEL ORTEGA	**LIED TO REAGAN**
DONALD T. REGAN	**GRAND TALE, DON**
GREGORY RASPUTIN	**PRYING ROGUE, TSAR!**
HAROLD WILSON	**LORDS NOW HAIL**
	AH, NO ILL WORDS
ALEXANDER FLEMING	**NEED AN ALL-GERM FIX**
DESDEMONA	**DAME'S DONE**
e. e. cummings	**SMUG, NICE ME**
DYLAN THOMAS	**HOT LADY'S MAN**
THOMAS HARDY	**AH-HA, MOST DRY!**
E. M. FORSTER	**TERSE FORM**
W. SOMERSET MAUGHAM	**WHO ME, A SMUG MASTER?**
JEAN-PAUL SARTRE	**JEERS UP AN ALTAR**
MARCEL PROUST	**CALM, PURE SORT**
IGOR STRAVINSKY	**SAVORY, STRIKING**
AARON COPLAND	**CODA RAN ON, PAL**
RICHARD WAGNER	**A HARD "RING," CREW**
JOAN SUTHERLAND	**JUST LAND ON HER "A"!**
MARILYN HORNE	**HER MANLY IRON**
STEPHEN SONDHEIM	**HE PENS DEMON HITS**
ANDREW LLOYD WEBBER	**BLEND OLD, WEARY BREW**
NEIL SIMON	**SMILIN' ONE**
OSCAR DE LA RENTA	**LENDS A RARE COAT**
PIERRE CARDIN	**ARDEN PRICIER**
DIANA VREELAND	**DIANA LAVENDER**

145

DONALD TRUMP	DOLT RAN DUMP
	DUMP DARN LOT
WALL STREET	SWELL TREAT
NORMAN MAILER	MINOR REAL MAN
WILLA CATHER	WHAT I RECALL
LAKE WOBEGON DAYS	BOY, A KEEN WAG SOLD
SAM DONALDSON	SLAMS AN ODD "NO"
TED TURNER	TRUE TREND
VANESSA REDGRAVE	SAD AVENGER RAVES
ALEC GUINNESS	SANG CUE LINES
HARRISON FORD	FINDS A HORROR
ROBERT DE NIRO	INERT BROODER
TOM CRUISE	SO I'M CUTER
MERYL STREEP	MY PERT LEERS
SIGOURNEY WEAVER	REVIEWS ANGER YOU

◆ MAGICAL CLERIGRAMS ◆

"Young Olivier's delivery
Will one day be silvery,"
Says my coach at drama school
Mouthing whom **I LEARN
VOICE RULE.**

LAURENCE OLIVIER

Maggie Smith
Uses elbows and hands to act
with.
And her voice is a positive
crime.
Won't someone please **GAG
THIS MIME?**

MAGGIE SMITH

Woody Allen
Drinks milk by the gallon.
In the hope that soon he
Won't be thought **A LEWD
LOONY.**   WOODY ALLEN

Ingmar Bergman
Is a Strindberg fan.
Notwithstanding, the studio
  planner
Asked him to **BAG GRIM
MANNER.**   INGMAR BERGMAN

Oedipus Rex
Denounced Mumsy, his ex.
"How low you made me stoop!
King was **I, OR SEX DUPE?**"   OEDIPUS REX

The Marquis de Sade
Applies too much pomade.
Just one reason, I claim,
He'd make a **SAD SQUIRE,
DAME.**   MARQUIS DE SADE

Isaac Newton
Left the part about the forbidden
  fruit in.
When told that that was no sign
Snapped, "I suppose you **WANT
A COSINE?**"   ISAAC NEWTON

Albert Einstein
Preferred, **"BITS RELATE,
NEIN?"**
He never really cared
For "$E = mc^2$."   ALBERT EINSTEIN

Louis Leakey
Is quoted as having been
  cheeky:
"When I find a dig gets dull
Then **O, I EYE A SKULL.**"   LOUIS LEAKEY

When speaking on matters
  Victorian
The Queen became rather
  stentorian.
After throwing the occasional fit,
She'd ask, **"O, CAN I EVER
  QUIT?"**   QUEEN VICTORIA

Nelson found honor at the Nile
(Then he decamped for a while).
But when he reduced the French
  to zero,
They cheered: **LO, NATION'S
  HERO!**   HORATIO NELSON

Basil Henry Liddell Hart
Was sure he'd told his men to
  start.
Then why were they all standing
  still?
And who on earth had **HALTED
  DRILL?**   LIDDELL HART

Thomas Paine
Hates the reign.
Against the king's men
He **AIMS A HOT PEN.**   THOMAS PAINE

General Cornwallis
At Yorktown finds no solace.
With its back against the walls
The imperial **LION CRAWLS.**   CORNWALLIS

The Boston Brahmin
Asked, "What's the hahm in
Being one, and not of the mob?
For **I'M HE, THAT BORN
  SNOB.**"   THE BOSTON BRAHMIN

Maria Callas,
Vowing vengeance and malice,
Shrieked, "I cannot do the gala
For they say **I MAR LA
  SCALA!**"   MARIA CALLAS

148

Noël Coward
In front of Porter cowered.
Although he never quite stole
He did in fact **DRAW ON COLE.**　　NOËL COWARD

Christie felt protective
Of her meddlesome detective
When she had to face
AH, AIRTIGHT CASE!　　AGATHA CHRISTIE

Anthony Trollope
Gave himself a wallop.
"To finish the damned lot
I need **ONLY ANOTHER
　　PLOT.**"　　ANTHONY TROLLOPE

Louella Parsons
Reveals all star sins.
How cruel her scrawl!
A SNOOP RULES ALL.　　LOUELLA PARSONS

Ludwig Mies van der Rohe
Stood his buildings all in a row.
Office drones spend their lives
In these **MODERN-ERA HIVES.**　　MIES VAN DER ROHE

Salvador Dali
Knew a touch of melancholy
When a critic from Granada
Wrote: **LO, RIVALS DADA.**　　SALVADOR DALI

Gertrude Stein
Called her publisher a swine.
He admitted he'd only read bits,
And now he wants **URGENT
　　RE-EDITS.**　　GERTRUDE STEIN

Alice B. Toklas
Yearned to be yokeless.
She'd say she was born in Ohio
To show Stein's **TALE LACKS
　　BIO.**　　ALICE B. TOKLAS

Marcel Proust
Needed a memory boost.
"*Allons,* let's pump it.
ALORS, CRUMPET!"   MARCEL PROUST

Madame Bovary—
Her husband made the
    discovery.
"The cause of your dilemma
May be a **BAD OVARY, EMMA.**   MADAME BOVARY

Marie Antoinette
Offered them *gateau noisette,*
'Twas rich and thick and terribly
    sweet
And cheap—**I.E., NO MEAT IN
    TREAT.**   MARIE ANTOINETTE

The Mona Lisa
Was put in the tower of Pisa.
During all this sad while
On her face **AH, NOT A SMILE.**   THE MONA LISA

Howard Cosell
Must be off his carousel.
Or maybe plumb out of his gourd
For he's asking, **"WHO-ALL
    SCORED?"**   HOWARD COSELL

Joe Namath
For shameth.
In that stockinged gam
You're **NO JET—A HAM!**   JOE NAMATH

◆ COUPLET-CROSTICS ◆

Note: The number of the couplet-crostic appears on the right-hand side of the page; the solution is on the left-hand side. This is so you can locate the solution you wish without inadvertently seeing the answers to other couplet-crostics.

Couplet-Crostic #1

Clue Words:
A.   LOOT
B.   ILLUSORY
C.   GAME
D.   HART CRANE
E.   TRUANCY
F.   VACUOUS
G.   ESTE
H.   RANDOMLY
I.   SCYLLA
J.   ELVES

First letters spell: "Light Verse"
Subject: OGDEN NASH
Quotation:
Octaves Galore, Dactyls Ever Numerous,
Nearly All Syntactically Humorous.

151

Clue Words:
A. DEARTH
B. EUCLID
C. PROXY
D. RIDDLE
E. ORBIT
F. FIGHT
G. UMLAUT
H. NCO
I. DANSE
J. IDIOTIC
K. SEESAW

First letters spell: "De Profundis"
Subject: OSCAR WILDE
Quotation:
Oafish Slander, Cried About, Recited,
With Impunity Lord Douglas Excited.

Clue Words:
A. ENMITY
B. VEDA
C. ORDNANCE
D. LORD
E. UNCLE SAM
F. THEO
G. INGRES
H. OCCIDENT
I. NEED
J. IPSWICH
K. SWELL
L. THIEF

First letters spell: "Evolutionist"
Subject: CHARLES DARWIN
Quotation:
Confirm How A Random Line Ends Selected.
(Discount Any Reptiles Which I've Neglected.)

Couplet-Crostic #4

Clue Word:
A.   HAROLD ARLEN
B.   ACTION
C.   UPJOHN
D.   TOT
E.   EVIAN
F.   CODA
G.   UTOPIA
H.   IRRIGATION
I.   SIZZLED
J.   IOTA
K.   NIGHTMARISH
L.   EPIGRAM

First letters spell: "Haute Cuisine"
Subject: JULIA CHILD
Quotation:
Jovial, Uproarious Legend In Aromatization
Chopping Haricots In Lighthearted Dramatization.

Couplet-Crostic #5

Clue Words:
A.   IND
B.   NHM
C.   THOMAS
D.   ENGLAND
E.   RAMADAN
F.   ESPY
G.   SADDLE
H.   THISTLE

First letters spell: "Interest"
Subject: ADAM SMITH
Quotation:
And Demand's All Master-planned
So Mighty Is The "Hand."

Clue Words:
A. SCREENING
B. WESTPHALIA
C. AFTERMATH
D. NON SEQUITUR
E. LOQUACIOUS
F. ABLER
G. KEEP
H. EINSTEIN

First letters spell: "Swan Lake"
Subject: MARIUS PETIPA
Quotation:
Makes All Rewhirl In Unison Statuesque,
Pointing Each Toe In Perfect Arabesque.

Clue Words:
A. CLOISTER
B. AVOWAL
C. RIDGE
D. A-B-C-D-E
E. VESTRY
F. AGREED
G. NORM
H. SHOVEL
I. ASTHMA
J. REDEEM
K. YELP

First letters spell: "Caravansary"
Subject: MARCO POLO
Quotation:
Mayhem And Riots, Camels Overweighted.
(Places Observed Largely Overrated.)

Clue Words:
A.   CHUNK
B.   OUSTER
C.   LOCK
D.   OPTION
E.   RANKE
F.   FAUST
G.   IMAGE
H.   ERDA
I.   LATCH
J.   DOCK

First letters spell: "Color Field"
Subject: MARK ROTHKO
Quotation:
Made A Rectangular Knockout.
(Replicas Of This He'd Knock Out.)

Clue Words:
A.   BRAVOS
B.   ISSUER
C.   LUGE
D.   LAERTES
E.   YEMEN
F.   WORSTED
G.   IGNOBLE
H.   LANCET
I.   DUNCAN

J.   ENSURE
K.   RATS

First letters spell: "Billy Wilder"
Subject: GRETA GARBO
Quotation:
Gentle Reclusive Endures Troubles Alone,
Grand Actress Remains Beauty's Own.

Couplet-Crostic #10

Clue Words:
A.   IN-LAW
B.   NOGGIN
C.   DEBS
D.   UTMOST
E.   STRANGLE
F.   TAMMANY
G.   REJOIN
H.   YEATS

First letters spell: "Industry"
Subject: JAMES WATT
Quotation:
Joy Abounds—My Engine Steams!
Warning All Trotting Teams.

Couplet-Crostic #11

Clue Words:
A.   NIGHT
B.   EQUINE
C.   WEPT
D.   AXEL
E.   MANET
F.   SITTING
G.   TURNIP
H.   EXTENT
I.   RENOIR

156

J.   DITCH
K.   ATHLETE
L.   MARY CASSATT

First letters spell: "New Amsterdam"
Subject: PETER MINUIT
Quotation:
Peremptory Exchange, This Exacting Requital.
Manhattan Is Netted, Unwritten Its Title.

Couplet-Crostic #12

Clue Words:
A.   MAHLER
B.   YOUNG
C.   SORROWS
D.   TRIFLE
E.   END RUN
F.   ROOFER
G.   IDYL
H.   EVANS
I.   SLAVING

First letters spell: "Mysteries"
Subject: NGAIO MARSH
Quotation:
New Goings-on, Affair Isn't Over.
Murderers All 'Round Slyly Hover.

Couplet-Crostic #13

Clues:
A.   SIEVE
B.   PROBITY
C.   ASHEN
D.   NETHER
E.   GUESTS
F.   LESSEN
G.   EXPIRE
H.   DIREST

157

First letters spell: "Spangled"
Subject: BETSY ROSS
Quotation:
"Best Enlarge These Six . . . Yipes!
Ruined Other Seven Stripes!"

Clues:
A.   DEMME
B.   USE
C.   BEJART
D.   LARYNX
E.   INDUS
F.   NILSSON
G.   EXAMEN
H.   ROMBERG
I.   SUBJECT

First letters spell: "Dubliners"
Subject: JAMES JOYCE
Quotation:
Jabber And Mumbling—Endless Stream.
Jinx On You, Curses Extreme!

Clues:
A.   OZAWA
B.   LETTERS
C.   YONKERS
D.   MENDES
E.   PANTHER
F.   INSIGHT
G.   ASPHALT
H.   NOSES

First letters spell: "Olympian"
Subject: MARK SPITZ

Quotation:
Mighty Athlete (Reason's Known)
Splashes Past In Treaders' Zone.

Clues:
A.   GREEN
B.   LAYERS
C.   INLET
D.   STASIS
E.   SUBTLE
F.   AZORES
G.   NATTY
H.   DELFT
I.   OUZO

First letters spell: "Glissando"
Subject: FRANZ LISZT
Quotation:
Fiery Runs And Notable Zest
(Legato Is Surely Zealot's Test).

Clues:
A.   GOTHIC
B.   ROOMY
C.   OWENS
D.   WIDOW
E.   TYPE
F.   HOLLYWOOD
G.   RIVULET
H.   APSE
I.   TACITUS
J.   EUCHRE
K.   SMARTS

First letters spell: "Growth Rates"
Subject: THOMAS MALTHUS

Quotation:
To Hold Overcrowding Must Await Species?
My, A Low Theory, How Utterly Specious!

Clues:
A. AMID
B. SHINGLE
C. SUDETEN
D. OGDEN
E. NIGHT
F. A JET
G. NINE
H. CHINK
I. EGGPLANT

First letters spell: "Assonance"
Subject: JOHN KEATS
Quotation:
Judgment On His *Nightingale:*
"Keep Ending And Tighten Scale."

PALINDROMES

1. STIFF FITS

2. BORROW, OR ROB?

3. I'D REVERE VERDI

4. WON KID, I KNOW

5. SINISTER FRET, SIN IS

6. TRADES USED ART
   (Also note: TRADED ART)

7. BORODIN I DO ROB

8. DRAW, ANIMATE . . . YET AM IN A WARD

9. DEB EXULTS: "A VAST, LUXE BED!"

10. AN AIDE BE DIANA

11. WALES, USE LAW!

12. DIAPER TOTAL A TOT REPAID

13. DEFINITE SET IN I FED

14. TIME, DID LOSE NO TIME . . .
    SEMITONES OLD I'D EMIT

15. SAME, NICE CINEMAS

16. MADE NILE PIPELINE DAM

17. REWARD STRAY ARTS DRAWER

18. DAMMIT, I'M MAD!

19. I MADE TASTE, YET SATED AM I